Handmade Christmas

Handmade Christmas

over 35 step-by-step projects and inspirational ideas for the festive season

CICO BOOKS
LONDON NEW YORK

Published in 2015 by CICO Books
An imprint of Ryland Peters & Small Ltd

20–21 Jockey's Fields   341 E 116th St
London WC1R 4BW   New York, NY 10029

www.rylandpeters.com

10 9 8 7 6 5 4 3 2 1

Text © Emma Hardy, Annie Rigg, Laura Tabor, Mia
Underwood, Catherine Woram, and Clare Youngs
Design and photography © CICO Books 2015

A CIP catalog record for this book is available from
the Library of Congress and the British Library.

ISBN: 978 1 78249 242 9

Printed in China

Designer: Geoff Borin
Art director: Sally Powell
Production controller: David Hearn
Publishing manager: Penny Craig
Publisher: Cindy Richards

contents

introduction

Christmas is the perfect time to indulge all your crafting skills, from making decorations for your home to thoughtful presents for friends and family. Creating something by hand, whether a gift or a greetings card, can be great fun, and it also shows how much you care.

The projects in this book for decorating your home include a simple-to-sew advent calendar, folk-art candle holders made from foil, crackers for your dining table, and a stunning gingerbread house. The Christmas tree is always the focal point, and handmade tree decorations soon become family heirlooms. Choose from paper hanging tassels, tin bird clips, a felt snowflake garland, and more. There are plenty of projects for making cards and giftwrap, too, plus ideas for gift tags, gift boxes, and goody bags.

Handmade gifts are always appreciated and here you will find simple recipes for Christmas cookies, chocolate money, and lebkuchen. If you enjoy sewing, try making the floral booties or the reindeer pillow. Many of the projects are perfect for children to make, too—choose from paper snowflakes, pompom decorations, potato print giftwrap, snow globes, and more.

Whether you enjoy baking, sewing, or papercrafting, you are sure to find this book packed with ideas for the perfect handmade Christmas.

CHAPTER I

decorations

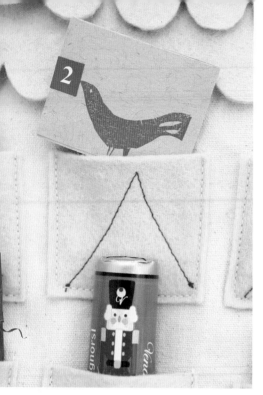

advent calendar

Traditionally, advent calendars are made from card with little windows to open each day to reveal a picture. This charming advent calendar, in the shape of a house, can be used year after year and personalized to suit the age and preferences of its recipients. Fill the tiny pockets with hand-picked treats. It doesn't have to be much—a wrapped candy, a small charm or gift, a picture, or a note. This is all you need to make it a very special countdown to Christmas.

Materials

Tracing paper or card

Pencil

Ruler

17¼ x 25¼ in. (44 x 64 cm) thick cotton or canvas

Scissors

Approx. 12 x 17¾ in. (30 x 45 cm) cream felt

Air-erasable pen

Sewing machine

Red cotton thread to match the canvas and sewing thread

Pins

7 in. (18 cm) ribbon for hanging loop

1 To make the template for front and back section, copy the roof section from the template on page 111. Continue the dotted line to measure 25 in. (64 cm) from the point of the roof. Continue the line on the other side of the oblong until it is the same length. Join together with a line to make the base of the oblong. Fold the piece of canvas in half, lay the template with the dotted line along the fold. Cut out the house shape and then repeat to make two identical pieces. Use the template to cut out the door and 24 oblongs each measuring 2 x 1¾ in. (5 x 4.5 cm), from the felt for the windows.

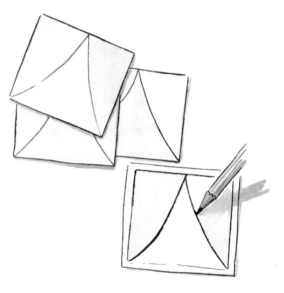

2 Transfer the drape (curtain) shape onto tracing paper. Cut the shape out and draw the drapes onto the 24 oblongs with an air-erasable pen. Machine stitch over the lines with red thread.

3 Copy the tile template on page 111 and transfer to tracing paper or card, then cut out. Draw around the template on the felt to make up four sections of roof tiles measuring 12½ in. (32 cm), 9½ in. (24 cm), 7 in. (18 cm), and 4¼ in. (11 cm) in length. Move the template along the felt to get the required length.

4 Pin the door in position, centered on the width and ½ in. (13 mm) up from the bottom edge. Next, position the windows in five rows. Start with the top row, positioning five windows so that their bottom edges are 10½ in. (27 cm) up from the bottom edge of the house. Leave a border of 1 in. (2.5 cm) on each side and space them out evenly. Pin in place. Position the other four rows evenly, finishing with the base of the last row of four windows, 1½ in. (4 cm) from the bottom edge.

5 Using matching thread, machine stitch around the two sides and base of each window to make a pocket. Keep the stitching close to the edge. Machine stitch the door, leaving the curve at the top unstitched to create a pocket.

6 Pin the longest section of tiles so that the top edge is 3 in. (8 cm) down from the roof top. Leave an equal overlap at each side and then machine sew in position with matching thread. Sew the remaining three sections of tiles, spacing them at ¾-in. (2-cm) intervals above each other. Trim the overlapping pieces of felt flush with the roof edge.

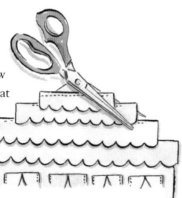

7 Pin the back and front house pieces together, with right sides facing. Fold the length of ribbon in half and tuck it inside at the top point of the roof, with the loop facing down inside. Leave the two ends sticking out and pin in place. Sew around the sides and roof, taking a ⅜-in. (1-cm) seam allowance, but leave the bottom edge open.

Make a date

To help keep track of the countdown you need to include the date, either on your wrapped gifts or attached to the pockets. Number stamps or stickers are perfect for adorning wrapped treats, or hand embroider numbers or stitch cut-out fabric numerals to each window. To keep the children guessing, place the numbered treats out of sequence.

8 Turn right sides out. Fold under a ½-in. (13-mm) hem along the bottom edge, pin, and top stitch along the edge to finish.

for kids: gingerbread house

Nothing says Christmas like a gingerbread house, and this one is straight out of a fairy tale. You could decorate the cake with any number and type of candies, so let your imagination run wild. Be aware that you will need to make up the recipe twice.

Ingredients

Make up this recipe twice:

3 cups (375 g) all-purpose (plain) flour, plus extra for dusting

½ teaspoon baking powder

1 teaspoon baking soda (bicarbonate of soda)

3 teaspoons ground ginger

½ teaspoon ground cinnamon

¼ teaspoon each of ground cloves and allspice

A pinch of salt

½ cup (125 g) unsalted butter, softened

⅓ cup (75 g) dark muscovado sugar

1 egg, lightly beaten

⅓ cup (100 ml) corn syrup (golden syrup)

2–3 cups (350–500 g) royal icing sugar

Assorted candies (sweets)

Serves 12

Equipment

Large sheet of baking parchment

Pencil

Metal rule

3 solid baking sheets, lined with baking parchment

Piping bag, fitted with a plain tip (nozzle)

1 Sift the flour, baking powder, baking soda (bicarbonate of soda), ginger, cinnamon, cloves, allspice, and salt together into a mixing bowl and set aside.

2 Put the butter and muscovado sugar in the bowl of an electric mixer (or use a large bowl and an electric whisk) and cream them together until fluffy.

3 Add the beaten egg and corn syrup (golden syrup) and mix until smooth. Add the sifted dry ingredients and mix again until smooth.

8

9

4 Sprinkle a little flour on a clean work surface. Shape the dough into a ball, then push on it and press it onto the work surface, turning it round often. Do this for a minute, then flatten into a disc, cover with plastic wrap (clingfilm), and chill for a couple of hours until firm.

5 Repeat steps 1–4 to make a second quantity of gingerbread dough.

6 When you are ready to bake the house, preheat the oven to 350°F (180°C/Gas 4).

7 You will need to make paper templates for the walls and roof of your house. Take a large sheet of baking parchment and draw a rectangle measuring 8 x 4¼ in. (20 x 11 cm) for the roof. Make another paper rectangle measuring 7½ x 4 in. (19 x 10 cm) for the front and back walls. You will also need a template for the sides—this will be a 4-in. (10-cm) square with a 1½ in. (4-cm) high triangle on top.

8 Sprinkle more flour on the work surface. Using a rolling pin, roll out the dough to a thickness of about ⅛ in. (3–4 mm). Use your paper templates to cut out 2 roof shapes, 2 big walls, and 2 sides. You may find it easier to write on the baking parchment which shapes are which as you cut them out.

9 Arrange the shapes on the prepared baking sheets. If you wish, carefully cut out windows from the walls and sides. Gather up any scraps of dough, knead very lightly to bring together into a ball, and roll out again to stamp out any other cookie shapes that you like.

10 Bake the gingerbread on the middle shelf in the oven for about 10–15 minutes until firm and just starting to brown at the edges. You will need to bake the gingerbread in batches. Remove from the oven and leave to cool completely.

11 Use the royal icing sugar to make icing according to the packet instructions. It will need to be thick enough to hold its shape when piped, so add the water gradually until you have the correct consistency. Fill the piping bag with the icing. You will need 2 pairs of hands for the next step!

12 Take one gingerbread side and pipe a line of icing along the bottom and up one side (just up to but not including the gables). Hold it up on a serving tray or platter. Take a big wall and pipe some icing along the bottom and 2 sides. Hold this at a right angle to the first, iced side. Pick up the second big wall and pipe some icing along the bottom and 2 sides. Hold this in place opposite the other wall and so that it meets the side at a right angle. Repeat with the remaining side. You may find it easier to position tins or jars inside the house to hold the walls in place until the icing has set firm.

13 To decorate the house, pipe royal-icing patterns onto the roof panels and decorate with your choice of candies (sweets). Pipe borders around the windows and doors, as well as along the bottom of the house, and decorate with candies (sweets) as you like.

14 Once the walls are completely set and secure, you can attach the roof. Pipe a line of icing down the gables and position one roof panel on either side of the gables. Pipe a line of icing across the top of the roof. Hold the roof in place until the icing feels firm, then decorate the ridge of the roof with extra candies (sweets).

christmas stockings

Hanging out the Christmas stocking is a tradition that children everywhere look forward to, and these stockings in traditional red and white are special enough to become family heirlooms, bulging with presents on Christmas morning. These instructions are for the appliquéd and embroidered reindeer stocking. For the snowflake and heart designs, use the stitch guides on page 113 for the embroidery and make up the stockings following the instructions below.

1 Enlarge the stocking template on pages 112–113 by 200 percent. Trace it onto the red fabric, and cut out the front and back of the stocking.

Materials

To make one reindeer stocking:

24-in. (60-cm) square of red felt or woollen fabric

Pencil

Scissors

7 x 9½ in. (18 x 24 cm) cream felt for appliqué

Pins

Embroidery needle

Red and white embroidery floss (thread)

18 in. (45 cm) black-and-white striped ribbon, 1½ in. (4 cm) wide

Sewing machine with matching thread

7 in. (18 cm) cream cotton tape or webbing for hanging loop

2 Enlarge the reindeer template on pages 112–113 by 200 percent. Trace it onto cream felt and cut out. Pin the reindeer in position on the front of the stocking. Following the stitch guide on the template, embroider the stitches on the reindeer. You do not need to sew around the very edges of the felt, as the decorative stitches secure it in place. Using running stitch, sew the trail.

3 With right sides together, place the front and back of the stocking together. Pin down the back seam until you reach the curve. Open up the stocking and pin the ribbon all along the top edge on the right side, overlapping the top by about ½ in. (1 cm). Machine stitch close to the bottom edge of the ribbon to attach it to the stocking.

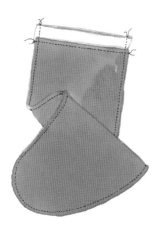

4 Trim the ends of the ribbon level with the edges of the stocking. With right sides together, fold the stocking back in half and machine stitch all around the sides, ½ in. (1 cm) from the edge. Trim the seam allowance to ¼ in. (5 mm) and turn the stocking right side out.

5 Fold the cotton tape or webbing in half lengthwise and pin it inside the stocking at the top of the back seam, leaving about 2 in. (5 cm) sticking up above the top of the stocking. Machine stitch a line of zigzag stitches across the raw edges of the tape and just below the top edge of the ribbon to make the hanging loop. Press.

for kids: paper snowflakes

Do you remember making snowflakes as a child and the pleasure of opening out the folds to see what they looked like? Although they are made with just a humble piece of white paper and a few snips with the scissors, there is something very special about them. Grouped together in a window, they make a charming display, or use them to create a garland for the Christmas tree. This is a really easy project so everyone can get involved—put on some Christmas music and get the kids snipping!

Materials

Sheets of white letter size (A4) paper

Tracing paper

Pencil

Scissors

Glue stick

Thread

1 Fold up the left bottom corner of the paper to line up with the right edge. Cut off the spare rectangle of paper. You can use this to make small squares for tiny snowflakes. Make several different size squares to vary the snowflakes.

2 Fold the triangle in half. Then fold it in half again.

3 Use the tracing paper and a pencil to transfer the snowflake design template on page 110 onto the folded paper triangle. Cut out the marked shapes. Instead of using the template, you could just snip away to make every snowflake different.

4 Open out the folded paper to reveal your snowflake.

5 Glue the snowflakes together in a row, to create a garland, or tie them together with thread to hang at different heights for a wintery window display.

tin candle holder

These unusual candle decorations are based on the Mexican folk art of tin ware. This is a very satisfying project to work on as it is so easy, with pleasing results in no time! You can buy thin tin or foil from craft suppliers, or simply use foil serving dishes that you can find easily in discount stores. The candle holders make great decorations for your Christmas table, or try lining them up on the mantlepiece, above a row of stockings.

Materials

Tracing paper

Pencil

Scissors

2 sheets of thick foil (available from craft supply stores or use a disposable foil roasting tray), measuring approx. 8¼ x 10 in. (21 x 25 cm)

Old ballpoint pen

3 candles

Strong double-sided tape or glue

3 small metal tart tins to place the candles in (you can use small glass candle holders, but make sure that anything you use is very stable)

1 Copy and enlarge the horse template and patterns on page 110 onto tracing paper and cut out the horse shape.

2 Lay the template on a piece of foil. Draw around the template with a ballpoint pen—an old one that has run out of ink is ideal. Press firmly to make a clear indented line (it may help to place the foil on a newspaper or magazine, as this will allow you to make a deeper indentation). Cut out the horse shape. Take care, as the edges are sharp, and do not use your best fabric scissors as the blades will blunt very easily.

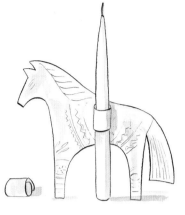

3 Lay the traced template on the foil horse and draw over the lines with the ballpoint pen, pressing firmly to transfer the pattern.

4 Place the horse next to the candle. Take a strip of foil approximately ¾ in. (2 cm) wide. Bend it into a ring and use double-sided tape or glue to stick it to the back of the horse, so that it fits snugly around the candle and the horse's feet are level with the bottom of the candle.

5 Repeat steps 1–4 to make the heart and circle decorations, using the templates on page 110. Place the decorated candle in the tart tin or holder. Repeat to make two more foil candle holders.

hanging tassels

These delicate baubles are lovely to make at Christmas. Hang them on painted silver and white twigs for a pretty and unusual festive display or add to your Christmas tree.

Materials

Pages from an old book (try to find thick paper for this project)

Cutting mat

Craft knife

Pencil

Ruler

Glue stick and glue

Bookbinder's awl or something with a sharp point such as a compass or metal skewer

Wire cutters

Thin wire (florists' or craft wire)

Scissors

Pair of pliers

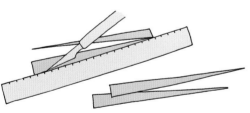

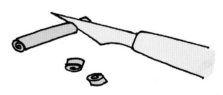

1 First make some paper beads. For one of the larger beads, cut a strip of paper the length of the page and ¾ in. (2 cm) wide. At one end of the strip make a pencil mark ⅜ in. (1 cm) in from the edge to mark the middle. With a ruler, join the top corner at the end of the strip to the pencil mark. Cut this section away and repeat on the other side to make a triangle.

2 Run the glue stick along the length of the triangle. Roll up the triangle starting at the wide end and keeping the roll tight. If you wish, you can vary the width of the triangles in order to get different-shaped beads.

3 Cut a strip of paper 1½ in. (4 cm) wide. Glue and roll it tightly in the same way as step 2. Using the craft knife, slice it into small sections measuring ¼ in. (5 mm) wide. These small beads are used to hold the strips of paper on the decoration in place

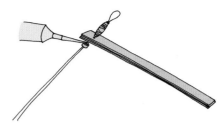

4 To make the bauble shape: cut out 15 strips of paper ⅝ x 6 in. (1.5 x 15 cm). Using the awl or other sharp point, make a small hole in the top of the strips, centered and approx. ⅓ in. (8 mm) from the edge. Place the strips together when making the holes so that the holes are in the same position on each strip. Repeat this at the other end of the strips.

5 Take a thin piece of wire, approx. 12 in. (30 cm) long, and fold it in half. Thread a larger bead onto the folded wire. You can push your sharp point through the bead first to make it easier. Position the bead about ⅝ in. (1.5 cm) from the end of the folded wire. Open out the loop of wire into a circular shape to stop the bead moving up any farther.

6 Thread all 15 strips of paper onto the folded wire. Take one of the small beads cut from the roll, thread it onto the wire, and push it up close to the strip of paper. Place a blob of glue on the end of the bead to secure it to the bottom strip of paper.

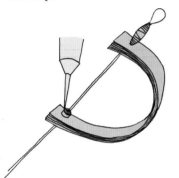

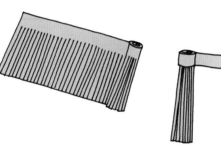

7 Thread another small bead onto the folded wire and then the other end of the strips of paper. Position the bead and strips of paper approx. 2 in. (5 cm) down the wire. Secure the bead to the strips and wire with a blob of glue, as in step 6.

8 Add another large bead to the wire and a small disc of paper measuring about ¾ in. (2 cm) in diameter.

9 To make the tassel: from a page, cut a rectangle of paper measuring 2 x 6 in. (5 x 15 cm). Using scissors, cut a fringe all along the width of the paper, stopping ½ in. (1 cm) from the other side (see illustration). Make the strips of the fringe about ¼ in. (5 mm) wide. Run a glue stick along the top edge of the fringe and roll up to form the tassel. Glue a ½ x 2 in. (1 x 5 cm) strip of paper around the top of the tassel for a neat finish.

10 Thread the tassel onto the wire. Use the small pair of pliers to bend the ends of wire over a few times to secure. Cut off any extra wire and hide the end of the wire among the tassels. Finally, open out the strips of paper to form a sphere. You can vary the shape of the decorations by changing the length of the strips of paper. You can also make double ones or even triple ones with different-sized spheres.

marzipan christmas figures

These sweet figures are perfect for decorating the Christmas table or even the top of the cake. Once you have decided which animal or shape to do, you can color your marzipan accordingly.

Ingredients

7 oz. (200 g) natural marzipan
Assorted food coloring pastes

Makes roughly 10 figures

To make one penguin

1 Break off a tiny piece of marzipan and tint it orange using the food coloring paste. Break off a satsuma-sized piece of marzipan from the block and tint it black. Break off a walnut-size piece and leave it white. Cover with plastic wrap (clingfilm).

2 Break off a cherry tomato-sized piece of black marzipan and roll into a ball for the penguin's head.

3 Reserve a tiny amount of white marzipan for the eyes. Roll the rest into a ball and put on the work surface for the body. Stick the black ball on top for the head.

4 Take a piece of the remaining black marzipan and flatten into a disc about the same width as the penguin's body, then stick it onto the back of the penguin.

5 Take 2 smaller pieces of black marzipan and shape into wing shapes. Attach to the side of the body.

6 For the feet, take 2 small nuggets of black marzipan, roll into balls, and flatten into oval discs. Press onto the bottom of the penguin's body so that they are clearly visible.

7 To make the eyes, take the reserved white marzipan, roll into 2 tiny balls, and flatten into discs. Roll 2 smaller balls of black marzipan into discs and stick in the middle of the white discs. Attach the eyes to the penguin's face.

8 Roll and pinch the orange marzipan into a beak shape. Stick this onto the penguin's face.

To make one reindeer

1 Break off 4 walnut-sized pieces of marzipan from the block. Add a bit of red food coloring to one piece of marzipan and knead it until the color is evenly mixed in. Repeat this process to tint the other pieces yellow and black. Leave the fourth piece white. Cover with plastic wrap (clingfilm).

2 Break off another piece of marzipan the size of a satsuma and tint it brown. Break off a piece of this slightly smaller than a walnut and roll into a ball. Break off another piece the size of a cherry tomato and roll into a ball. Stick onto the larger piece, slightly forwards for the head. Roll 6 small nuggets of brown marzipan into balls. Flatten 2 of them and stick to the top of the head for the ears. Attach the remaining 4 around the body for legs.

3 Roll a small nugget of red marzipan into a ball and attach to the face for the nose.

4 To make the eyes, break off 2 tiny pieces of white marzipan, roll into balls, and flatten into discs. Roll 2 smaller balls of black marzipan into discs and stick in the middle of the white discs. Attach the eyes to the reindeer's face.

5 Break off 2 small nuggets of yellow marzipan and shape roughly into antlers. Attach to the top of the head.

To make one snowman

1 Break off a small walnut-sized piece of marzipan from the block and tint it red using the food coloring paste. Take a slightly smaller piece of marzipan and tint it black with the food coloring. Tint another tiny piece orange. Cover with plastic wrap (clingfilm).

2 Break off another piece of marzipan the size of a satsuma. Divide this in 2—one piece slightly larger than the other. Roll both into balls and put the larger one on the work surface for the body. Stick the smaller ball on top for the head.

3 Roll the red marzipan into a thin snake and wrap this carefully around the snowman's neck for a scarf.

4 To make the eyes and buttons, break off 4 tiny pieces of black marzipan. Roll into balls and stick 2 of each onto the face and body.

5 Roll the orange marzipan into a carrot shape for the nose. Stick this in the middle of the snowman's face.

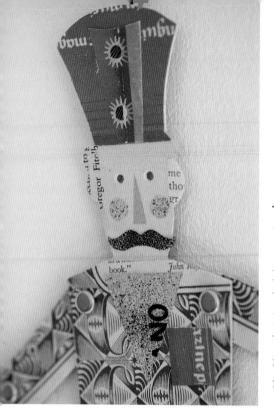

jumping jacks

Dust jackets on old books often get very tattered but the designs can be wonderful, with repeat patterns in gorgeous festive colors. Transform odd scraps into these delightfully old-fashioned Jumping Jacks—pull the string to make them jump. A row of these dancing Cossacks would make a quirky display.

Materials

Tracing paper

Pencil

Thin card

Scissors

Scraps of colored paper from book dust jackets

Glue

Cutting mat

Craft knife

Bookbinder's awl or something sharp to make holes (such as a hole punch)

Split craft pins

String or waxed cotton thread

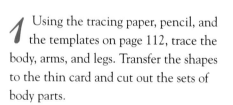

1 Using the tracing paper, pencil, and the templates on page 112, trace the body, arms, and legs. Transfer the shapes to the thin card and cut out the sets of body parts.

2 Cover the body parts with different scraps of paper from the colorful dust jackets. To do this, first cut out a piece of paper that is slightly larger than the body part. Cover the back of each piece of paper with a thin layer of glue, and then lay the thin card body part in position on the glued paper. Cut around the edge of each body part with the craft knife to remove the excess paper.

3 Using the tracing paper and templates on page 112, trace and cut out the facial features, then glue them into place. Use an awl or hole punch to make the eyes.

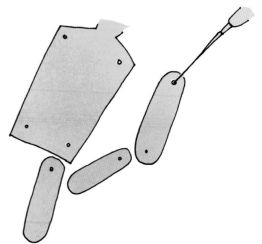

4 Use the awl or hole punch to make holes in the body and limbs following the templates as a guide. The holes should be large enough to fit a split craft pin.

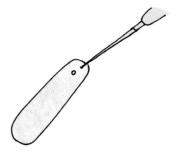

5 Make another slightly smaller hole between the first hole and the top edge of both upper arms and upper legs. (You will be threading the string through these.)

6 Join all the pieces together with the split craft pins, making sure that the arms and legs can move freely. Cover the boots and glove pieces with colorful paper and stick them in position.

7 Thread a piece of string or thread, approx. 4¾ in. (12 cm) long, through one hole at the top of the arm and up through the hole on the other arm. If you find this difficult to do with the arms clipped in position, slip them out of the split craft pins and then reposition.

8 Tie the two ends of string or thread together so that a loop is formed between the two arms. The loop should be neither too loose nor too tight. Tie it with the arms in a down position and test to see that if you pull the loop in the middle, pinching both bits of string, the arms will move up.

9 Do the same for the legs (repeat steps 7 and 8). Then take a piece of string approx. 12 in. (30 cm) long and tie it first around the top loop centered between the two arms and then around the loop between the two legs. You may need to adjust the strings to get the tension right.

for kids: pompom decoration

Pompoms are fun and easy to make, and you can use them to create cute Christmas tree baubles. Alternatively, you could make two different-sized pompoms and glue them together to make a snowman or robin, or even a Father Christmas figure complete with felt hat!

Materials

Paper

Pencil

Scissors

Thick card

Assorted balls of knitting yarn

Red 3-D fabric pen

Approx. 4 in. (10 cm) gingham
   ribbon per bauble

1 Trace the disc template on page 112 onto paper and cut it out. Place it on a piece of card and draw round it twice. Cut out the two discs and place them together. Cut a length of yarn about 2.2 yd (2 m) long and wind into a small ball that will fit through the hole in the discs. Start to wind yarn around the discs, binding them together. When the ball of yarn is finished, tie the end to the beginning of a new one. Continue to wind yarn round the discs until they are completely covered.

2 When the winding process is complete, hold the pompom discs securely and cut around the edges of the yarn using scissors. The yarn will fall away looking like fringing at this point, so it is important that the two discs are firmly held together.

3 Cut two lengths of yarn about 8 in. (20 cm) long and thread between the two cardboard discs. Pull them together tightly and knot tightly. The loose ends of this yarn will form the hanging loop for the decoration, so tie another knot about 3¼ in. (8 cm) from the first knot and neatly trim the ends.

4 Gently pull the cardboard discs away from the pompom. If it proves difficult, just cut them off. Trim any excess bits of yarn, and fluff the pompom to give it a nice round shape. Use a 3-D fabric pen to draw tiny dots on the pompom and finish with a length of red gingham ribbon tied in a bow around the hanging loop.

tealight houses

These pretty tealight houses have a simple but stylish Scandinavian look that is very appealing. Set the finished row of houses up on the mantelshelf with a tealight behind each house section—the open windows and doors will be lit with a warm glow, making a charming display.

Materials

Tracing paper

Pencil

9 x 20 in. (22 x 50 cm) thin white card

Scalpel or craft knife

Cutting mat

Metal rule

Tealights

1 Enlarge the template on pages 114–115 by 200 percent. With tracing paper and a pencil, trace the template and carefully transfer the outline onto the thin white card.

2 Using a scalpel or craft knife, cut out the outline of the houses. Cut out the windows and decorations on the houses, taking care not to cut the indicated score lines.

3 Score the fold lines where indicated and fold back. Score down between each house.

4 Fold one house forward and one house back to make a corrugated row of houses. Place a tealight behind each house at a safe distance.

tin bird clips

Christmas wreaths can decorate the inside as well as the outside of your home, and this beautiful but simple one, entwined with ivy sprigs, is perfect to hang above the fireplace. Little silver tin birds attached to wooden clips sit perched among the foliage and berries. Make a whole flock and clip them to the tree, to gifts, to napkins, or place holders—the possibilities are endless!

Materials

Tracing paper

Pencil

Scissors

Small piece of aluminum foil from a disposable roasting tray

Old ballpoint pen

Wooden clothes pins (pegs) or clips

Strong double-sided tape or glue

For the wreath:

Moss from a florist

Wire wreath base

Thin wire

Foliage

Silver leaves and decorations

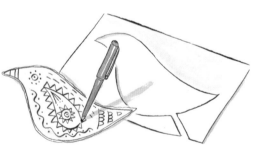

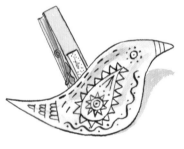

1 To make the foil bird clips, copy the bird template and pattern on page 114 onto tracing paper and cut out the shape.

2 Place the bird shape on a piece of foil and draw around it with a ballpoint pen—an old one that has run out of ink is ideal. Press firmly to indent the tin.

3 Cut out the bird shape. Take care, as the edges are sharp, and do not use your best fabric scissors as the blades will blunt very easily! Lay the traced template back on the foil bird and trace the patterns with the ballpoint pen, pressing firmly.

4 Attach the bird to the front of a wooden clothes pin (peg), using strong double-sided tape or glue. Repeat steps 1–4 to make as many birds as required.

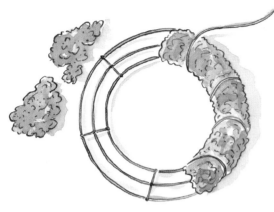

5 To make the wreath, take some moss and start wrapping and pressing it around the wire wreath base. Use thin wire to secure it in place.

6 Place the foliage around the wreath by poking it into the moss and securing with wire. Add some silver leaves or strands of small silver decorations for a little sparkle. Clip the foil birds into position amongst the leaves and add a loop of wire to the back to hang.

snowflake garland

*Red-and-white decorations are always a stylish choice at
Christmas. This simple Nordic-inspired garland, embroidered
on felt and strung along a bright red cord or ribbon, will add
a touch of Scandinavian charm to your mantelshelf or tree.
Keep accessories simple and, if you wish add some foliage for
a look that is rustic but modern.*

Materials

Pencil

Paper

Scissors

Pins

Approx. 4 x 4 in. (10 x 10 cm) thick
   white felt for each star

Air-erasable pen or dressmaker's pencil

Dressmaker's carbon paper

2.2 yd (2 m) red cord, ribbon,
   or felt string

Red embroidery floss (thread)

Embroidery needle

Sewing needle and matching thread

1 Copy the star template and stitch pattern (there is a choice of two
patterns) on page 114 onto paper and cut out the shape. Pin the
template to the felt. Use an air-erasable pen to draw around the star
shape and cut out. Cut as many stars as you want for your garland.

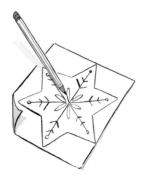  

2 Put a sheet of dressmaker's carbon paper on top of the felt star shape, with the colored, carbon side face down. Place the star template on top. Draw over the design with a pencil to transfer the embroidery pattern onto the felt.

3 Using red or contrasting embroidery floss (thread) and following the stitch guide on the template, embroider the pattern on to the felt star (see pages 107–109 for stitch instructions). This transforms the star into a pretty snowflake.

4 Position the finished stars along the length of cord at 15¾-in. (40-cm) intervals, sewing in place with matching thread. Make two loops in between each star and secure with a couple of stitches.

christmas crackers

Homemade crackers add a unique festive touch to your Christmas table setting. You can choose the paper to fit your scheme—and you get to pick the gifts that go inside! You can buy little charms or place a small, different decoration in each cracker. It is traditional for the cracker to contain a paper hat and a joke, but you can always decide to break with tradition and write a personal message instead!

Materials

Sheet of giftwrap or wallpaper
  (not too thick)

Cardboard tubing, approx. 1½ in.
  (4 cm) in diameter

Craft knife

Cutting mat

Double-sided tape, ⅜ in. (1 cm) wide

Cracker pulls

Gifts, hats, jokes, etc.

String

Ribbon or trimming

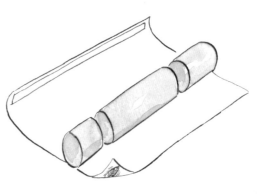

1 To make one cracker, cut an oblong of giftwrap measuring 6¼ x 11 in. (16 x 28 cm). Cut three sections of cardboard tube, one measuring 4 in. (10 cm) long and two measuring 2½ in. (6.5 cm) long.

2 Lay the giftwrap, pattern side down, on the work surface. Place a strip of double-sided tape across the width of the edge furthest away from you. Line up the three pieces of tube across the middle of the oblong. The two smaller pieces line up with the edge of the oblong and the longer piece is centered between them. Leave a small gap in between the larger and smaller tubes.

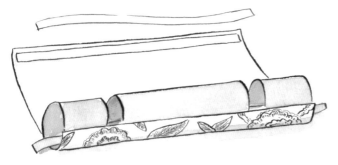

Personal touches

To help identify each cracker when matching it to your seating plan, add a matching name label to the cracker. This is especially important if you have chosen individual gifts to suit each recipient.

3 Place the cracker pull in the tubes so that it emerges equally on each end. Put the gift and anything else in the middle tube. Peel the backing from the double-sided tape and roll the paper around the tubes until the edges overlap. Press along the double-sided tape strip to secure in place.

4 Wrap a small piece of string around the paper in the gap between the large and small piece of tube on one side. Overlap the string and pull slowly and firmly. Remove the string and the small end tube. Repeat for the opposite end of the cracker. Keep the small tubes to use for the next cracker.

5 Tie a piece of ribbon or trimming to the cracker to finish. If using ribbon around the ends, don't tie it too tightly or the cracker may not pull apart successfully.

stained glass cookies

These stained-glass style snowflake cookies can be made in a rainbow of festive colors and look beautiful hung in a window to catch the light—the perfect edible Christmas decoration.

Ingredients

1 package boiled candies in assorted colors

For the vanilla cookies

Heaped ¾ cup (185 g) unsalted butter, softened

1¼ cups (240 g) superfine (caster) sugar

1 egg

1½ teaspoons vanilla extract

4 cups (390 g) all-purpose (plain) flour

½ teaspoon salt

Makes 12 cookies

Equipment

A non-stick baking sheet, greased

Snowflake cookie cutter set

Toothpicks

Icing tip (nozzle)

Small palette knife

Ribbon, for hanging

1 To make the cookies, beat the butter for a couple of minutes, then add the sugar and beat well until combined. Add the egg and vanilla extract and beat until creamy.

2 Sift the flour and salt into a bowl, then add one half of it to the butter mixture and beat until combined. Add the rest of the flour and mix for a few minutes until a dough begins to form and easily comes loose from the sides of the bowl.

3 Lightly flour your work surface. Turn the dough out and knead into a ball. Wrap in plastic wrap (clingfilm) and refrigerate for at least 30 minutes. Preheat the oven to 325°F (160°C/Gas 3).

4 Let your dough stand to soften up slightly, then roll it out on a lightly floured surface to an even thickness of ¼ in. (3–4 mm). Transfer to the prepared baking sheet. It's easier to cut out the detail on the cookies on the sheet, as they will be too delicate to move later. Cut out the snowflake shapes and then, using the small insert cutters, cut out snowflake patterns. Remove any stubborn pieces of dough with a toothpick. Use the icing tip (nozzle) to cut out a hole at the top of the snowflake; this will be used to thread the ribbon. Put the cookies in the fridge for 10 minutes, then part-bake the cookies for 6 minutes. Let cool on the baking sheet.

5 Put the boiled candies into separate sealed bags according to colors and smash with a rolling pin. Take care as the sweets will be hard, so use an old rolling pin or similar on a sturdy surface that will not mark.

6 Fill each of the snowflake cavities with pieces of smashed candy. Don't pile them too high. Pop the cookies back into the oven for a further 5–6 minutes. Remove from the oven. The "glass" parts will be bubbly, but the bubbles disappear as they cool. Leave the snowflakes on the sheet to cool for at least 20 minutes. With a small palette knife, gently slide under the cookies and lift each one off the sheet and let cool on a cooling rack. Tie each cookie with a ribbon to hang on your tree.

christmas coronets

A Nordic Christmas would not be the same without "coronets," also known as cornettes or "kræmmerhus." You can make them any size you like, from large ones to hang at the end of the bed instead of stockings, or lots of small ones to use as an advent calendar, or as decorations. Fill with candy, or tiny presents!

Materials

Tracing paper or card

Scissors

Cotton fabric of your choice,
    e.g., dots or gingham

Plain cotton fabric, for lining

Rikrak, bias tape, or ribbon

Sewing machine with matching thread

Pencil

1 Copy and enlarge the template on page 115 onto tracing paper or card, and use it to cut out one piece of fabric for the outside, and another for the lining of the coronet.

2 Cut a length of rikrak, bias tape, or ribbon for the handle about 5 in. (13 cm) long. Pin the handle to the top of the inside fabric shape on the right side, about 2 in. (5 cm) in from the edge on both sides (as marked on the template).

3 Place the main fabric piece over the lining piece, with right sides together. Using a sewing machine threaded with matching thread, sew across the top using straight stitch, about ¼ in. (1 cm) from the top, attaching the handle as you sew.

4 Open up the triangles, and then fold them in half lengthways with right sides facing. Sew over the edges, leaving a small gap of about 2 in. (5 cm) halfway down the lining, through which you then turn the coronet right side out. You may need to use a pencil to help push out the fabric in the point of the coronet. Sew the gap closed using slip stitch.

CHAPTER 2

cards & giftwrap

glittery bird card

Here a simple bird motif has been enhanced with glittery papers and ribbons and plumes of silver tissue paper. For a Christmassy look, choose metallic papers, or try a selection of co-ordinating papers in browns and reds for a subtle effect or bright colors for a modern look.

Materials

Thin cream card	Metal rule	Silver and gold ribbon, about ⅛ in. (3 mm) wide
Pencil	Gold and silver giftwrap	Silver crepe paper
Scissors	Glittery or patterned paper	Fast-drying, high-tack craft glue
Scalpel or craft knife	Glue stick	Gold star sequins
Cutting mat	Pinking shears	

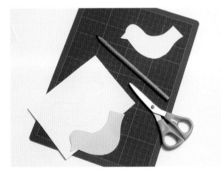

1 Copy the template on page 116, cut out, and lay onto cream card. Carefully draw around the template and cut out neatly with sharp scissors or a craft knife.

2 Cut a beak in metallic paper and a semi-circular wing in glittery paper. Glue the beak onto the bird. Fold over the straight edge of the wing, apply a thin line of glue, and stick the wing in position. Using pinking shears, cut two strips of metallic paper ½ in. (1cm) wide and glue across the neck and tail. Stick ribbon on top.

3 Cut two 1¼ x 2¾ –in. (3 x 7-cm) strips of silver crepe paper. Gather them along one long edge, holding firmly to crease them slightly. Using craft glue, glue one onto the back of the bird at the head and one at the tail. Hold in place until firmly stuck. Glue a sequin onto the bird for the eye.

4 Measure and cut out a 4 x 5½-in. (10 x 14-cm) rectangle of glittery paper. Measure and cut an 8½ x 6-in. (22 x 15.25-cm) rectangle of cream card, score centrally 4¼ in. (11 cm) from each side, and fold in half.

5 Apply the glue stick to the back of the glittery rectangle and stick onto the front of the card. Glue the bird into the center of this and glue ribbon around the edge of the glittery paper, ensuring a straight finish.

christmas stocking cards

Give a Christmas stocking with a difference. These cards will add festive cheer to any mantelpiece. Using a traditional Christmas color scheme of red and white, they make the perfect card for a child but will be equally loved by adults, too. Use store-bought giftwrap papers or decorate plain red and white card with adhesive stickers. The addition of ribbon and braid finishes the cards off beautifully.

Materials

Pencil

Scissors

Thin red and white card

Red and white circular stickers

Red and white patterned giftwrap

Glue stick

Red crepe paper

Sewing needle and red thread

Fast-drying, high-tack craft glue

Selection of braids and ribbons

Rotary hole punch

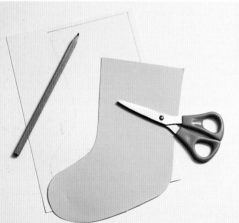

1 Copy and enlarge the stocking template on page 116. Using the template, draw and cut out stocking shapes from the white and red card.

2 For the spotted stockings, stick circular stickers randomly all over one side of the card stocking. Alternatively, draw around the template onto patterned paper and cut out. Glue this onto a plain card stocking with glue stick.

3 Cut a 12 x 1-in. (30.5 x 2.5-cm) strip of crepe paper. Stitch along one long edge, securing the thread with a knot at the start. Pleat the paper as you go by gathering it until it measures 4⅜ in. (11 cm). Finish with a few stitches or a knot.

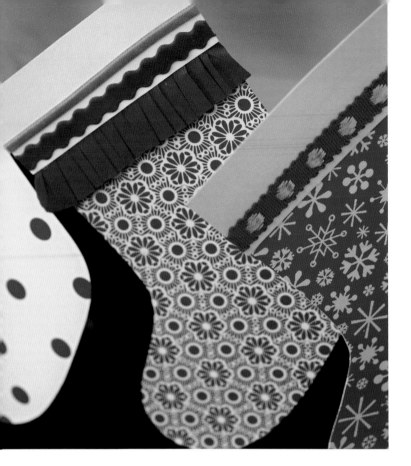

Tip

Make a large quantity of these pretty stocking cards and send one to each member of the family so they can be suspended in one long line above the fireplace as festive decorations.

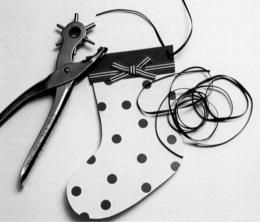

4 Cut out a cuff from either red or white card (the opposite color to the main stocking). Apply craft glue along the bottom of the cuff and glue the crepe paper ruffle along this, if using.

5 Glue the cuff onto the stocking. Decorate the tops of the stockings with lengths of ribbon and braid, adding a ribbon bow if desired.

6 Using the hole punch, make a hole in the top corner of the stocking. Cut a 6-in. (15-cm) length of thin red ribbon and thread it through the hole. Tie a neat knot in the ribbon and trim the ends to even them.

robin's nest card

Small buttons make a lovely embellishment for homemade cards. Pearl buttons like these can be expensive to buy, but look out for them in thrift stores and flea markets. Old music scores and labels used for the little bird give this holiday card a real vintage feel.

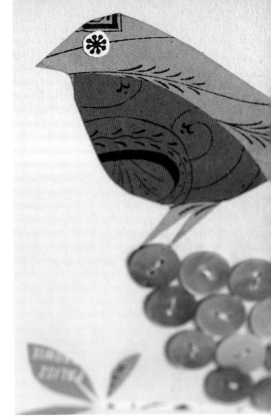

Materials

18 x 12 in. (45 x 30 cm) thin blue card

Pencil

Metal rule

Scalpel or craft knife

Cutting mat

Tracing paper

Selection of small buttons

Sewing needle and thread

Sheets of printed and colored paper

Glue

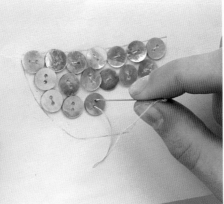

1 Cut out a piece of card measuring 5½ x 5½ in. (14 x 14 cm). Trace the nest template on page 117 and use it to mark out the area for the nest.

2 Sew buttons onto the piece of card to fill in the drawn outline of the nest shape.

3 Trace the templates for the robin, leaves and twigs on page 117 and transfer the outlines to interesting areas of the printed paper, then cut them out. Cut the robin's breast from a piece of red paper.

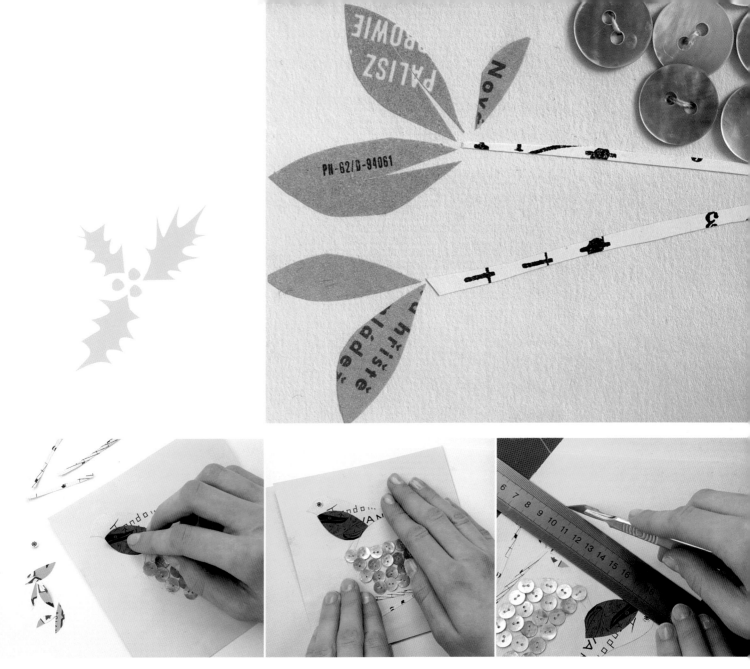

4 Stick down the robin, breast, twigs, and leaves in position on the front section of the card.

5 Cut out an oblong of card measuring 5½ x 11 in. (14 x 28 cm). Stick the decorated front section to the right-hand side of the oblong card.

6 Score down the center of the oblong with the back of the scalpel at the edge of the decorated section and fold it over to complete the card.

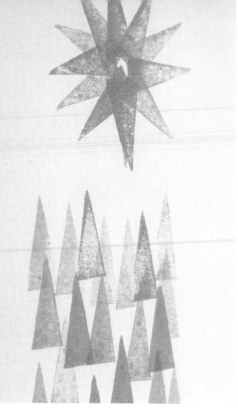

rubber-stamped cards

Making your own rubber stamps is an easy way to create original cards and giftwrap. Once cut, they keep for ever. Put together a collection to make endless combinations of patterns and designs. Look out for ink pads in unusual colors—metallic bronzes and silvers are perfect for Christmas.

Materials

Tracing paper

Pencil

White erasers, approx. 2 x ¾ in. (5 x 2 cm)

Craft knife

Cutting mat

Sheet of thin white card

Rubber stamping ink pads in assorted colors

Luggage labels

Sheets of thin white paper or brown parcel paper

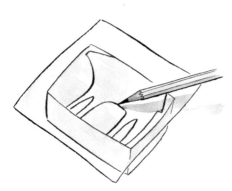

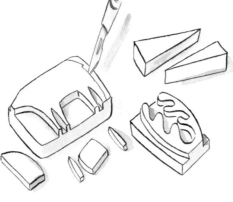

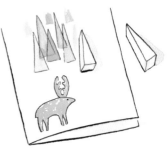

1 Copy the templates on page 117 onto tracing paper using a soft pencil. Place the trace on the eraser and transfer the pattern. Go over the lines with a sharp pencil, to make them clearer.

2 Use a craft knife to cut away a horizontal slice of the background, leaving the pattern standing proud by approx. ⅛ in. (3 mm). For the triangles, simply cut the whole triangle out, making sure you have sharp edges and points.

3 To make the card, fold a piece of white card measuring 6¾ x 7½ in. (17 x 19 cm) in half. Load the reindeer body stamp with ink and print a reindeer approximately ⅝ in. (1.5 cm) up from the bottom edge. Print the antlers in place. Use the triangle stamp to make a forest above the reindeer. Clean the stamps in warm water before changing colors. Print the larger triangle in a circle to make the sun.

4 To make gift labels and wrap, print up some luggage labels. Make rows of repeat patterns in different combinations on white paper or brown parcel paper. To make a reverse star shape, transfer the design onto an eraser. As you cut the spokes of the stars, angle the blade inward at a slant. Then cut from the other side of the spoke, sloping the blade toward the middle so that you cut out a "V" shape.

for kids: felt motif cards

Felt is great for decorating cards, as it comes in a wide selection of colors and does not fray once it is cut. You can use Christmas-themed cookie cutters as templates for a variety of festive designs. Glue the felt shapes onto stiff card and finish them off with dainty bows.

Materials

Round cookie cutter

Felt squares

Pencil

Scissors

Gingham ribbon, ¼ in. (6 mm) wide

Glue

Blank cards

Variations

As well as the round baubles, use simple shapes such as Christmas trees, stars, stockings, and birds. The template section at the back of the book can also be used.

1 Use the circular cookie cutter (or a similar object) as a template for the round bauble shape on this card. Place it on the felt and draw round it with a pencil. Carefully cut out the bauble shape. If you are making more than one card, it's a good idea to cut out all your felt shapes at the same time.

2 Cut a piece of gingham ribbon approx. 2 in. (5 cm) long and fold it into a loop. Glue the ribbon onto the card just below where the top of the bauble will be positioned. Press down firmly to secure it in place.

3 Apply a thin layer of glue to the back of the felt bauble shape and stick it onto the card, making sure that you have covered both the ends of the ribbon loop. Press down firmly and allow to dry completely.

4 Make a ribbon bow from the gingham ribbon. Apply a small dab of glue to the back of the bow, and stick to the front of the bauble. Press down firmly to secure it in place and leave to dry completely.

embroidery gift tags

These embroidered gift tags are based on traditional Swedish folk-art motifs. They may seem rather elaborate for labels, but they can be hung on the Christmas tree to be enjoyed year after year.

Materials

Pencil

Small pieces of red, green, pink, and cream felt

Scissors

Small pieces of thin card

Rotary hole punch

Embroidery needle

Brightly colored embroidery floss (thread)

Fabric glue

Lengths of ribbon, ⅛ in. (3 mm) wide, for hanging loops

1 Copy the tag templates on page 118. Trace them onto felt and cut out. Cut pieces of thin card to match the tags. Hold the card and felt tag shapes together and cut or punch a hole for the ribbon at the top of each one.

2 Set the card shapes to one side. Place the cut-out felt pieces on the tags. You do not have to sew them down, as the embroidery over the top holds them in position. Using the stitch guides on the templates, embroider each tag (see pages 107–109 for stitch instructions).

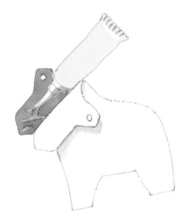

3 Using fabric glue, stick the card shapes to the back of the corresponding felt tag shapes, making sure that the holes for the ribbon align.

4 Cut small lengths of ribbon. Thread the ribbon through the hole in each tag and tie a knot to make a hanging loop.

goody bags and labels

Homemade candies and cookies make great Christmas gifts, and what better way to present them than in these traditional brown paper bags decorated with stitched hearts and gingerbread man labels? Their simple old-fashioned charm is given a festive touch with red-and-white ribbons. Some sewing machines have a choice of decorative stitches, but you could use a simple zig zag stitch for an equally pretty effect.

Materials

Thick brown paper

Craft knife

Cutting mat

Metal rule

Glue or double-sided tape

Decorative-edged scissors

Tracing paper

Pencil

Thin brown card

Hole punch

Sewing machine and red thread

String

Thin white card

Ribbon

1 To make a bag, cut a brown paper oblong 10 x 7½ in. (25 x 19 cm). Fold a strip ⅜ in. (1 cm) wide along one side edge. Fold the oblong in half, then open out. Cut a ⅜-in. (1-cm) strip from the bottom edge of the side that does not have the folded edge.

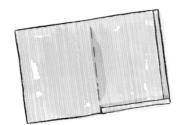

2 Fold the bottom edge of the side with the folded edge in by ⅜ in. (1 cm).

3 Place double-sided tape or apply glue to the two flaps. Fold the oblong in half, aligning the side and bottom edges. Press to seal the edges.

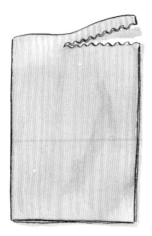

cookie surprise

These goody bags are perfect for wrapping a matching gingerbread man cookie! Make a batch of gingerbread dough following the recipe on page 14 and cut out the gingerbread shapes using the card templates. Once cooled, pop them inside the bags and adorn with a matching label.

4 Use decorative-edged scissors to cut a corrugated or patterned edge along the top of the bag.

5 To make the gingerbread labels, copy the templates on page 119 and cut out the shapes from thin brown card. Use a hole punch to cut out the eyes and make a hole to thread a tie through. Cut a mouth, using a craft knife.

6 Machine stitch a few lines of decorative stitching across the width of the gingerbread men and ladies. Thread a length of string through the hole to attach to gifts

7 Follow steps 5–6 to make the heart labels from white card. You can punch a hole to thread a ribbon through or you can tuck the heart into a ribbon tied around the bag.

8 To make the oblong label, cut a piece of white card 4¼ x 2½ in. (11 x 6.5 cm). Cut along one edge with decorative-edged scissors. Sew a line of zig zag stitching ⅝ in. (1.5 cm) in from the decorative edge. Cut out the heart shape in the lower half of the label with a craft knife.

patchwork wrap & card

You can make wonderful original giftwrap out of scraps from the recycling box; collect bits of paper throughout the year, such as old labels, bits of packaging, stamps and envelopes, paper bags, and old comics. You can personalize the wrap for individual members of your family or your friends, with photographs and their initials cut from magazines.

Materials

Sheet of brown paper (or an old sheet of giftwrap)

Scraps of labels, stamps, envelopes, graph paper, etc.

Glue

Sheet of thin white card

Metal rule

Pencil

Craft knife

Cutting mat

Tracing paper

Scraps of plain brown and red paper

Hole punch

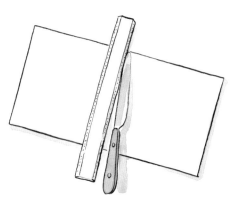

1 To make the gift-wrap, first wrap your present in a layer of brown paper or a sheet of old giftwrap. Cut out lots of scraps of paper in different-sized oblongs and start sticking them on like patchwork to cover the base layer.

2 To make the greetings card, cut an oblong of white card measuring 6 x 12 in. (15 x 30 cm). Mark the halfway point on the top and bottom edges. Join these two marks, score, and then fold the card in half.

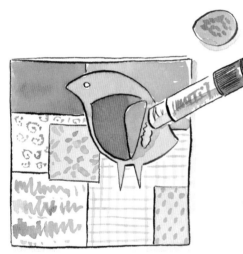

3 Cover the front of the card with scraps of envelopes and graph paper for the background. Copy the templates on page 117 and cut out the three sections of the bird. Use plain brown and red paper for the first two sections and a scrap from an envelope for the circle on the wing. Punch out a hole for the eye. Position the bird ⅜ in. (1 cm) in from the right edge and glue in place.

4 To make the mini envelope in the bird's mouth, cut out a small envelope shape. Fold in the two side flaps, glue them, and fold the back section of the envelope over so that the sides of the back section align with the glued flaps.

5 Fold over the top flap of the envelope, but don't stick this part down; you need to keep it open so that you can place a little Christmas message inside!

for kids: potato print giftwrap

Potato printing is a traditional painting technique that is a favorite with kids of all ages. They can use cookie cutters to create pretty shapes, or an adult could use a sharp knife to cut out different shapes by hand. Use with metallic paint for a festive giftwrap.

Materials

Medium-sized potato

Star-shaped cookie cutter

Chopping board

Sharp knife

Paper towels or dry cloth

Paints

Saucers to hold the paints

Sponge paint roller

Plain white paper

1 Cut the potato in half, making sure the surface of the potato is as flat as possible. Place the cookie cutter on a cutting board with the sharp edge facing upwards. Press the potato firmly down onto the cutter, leaving the cookie cutter standing proud of the cut surface of the potato by about ¼ in. (5 mm), so you can cut around it.

2 Cut away the edges of the potato using a sharp knife. This needs to be done very carefully, to ensure the star shape is as clear as possible. Press the potato down onto a dry cloth or paper towels to remove any excess moisture, which can make the paint watery.

3 Pour the paint into a saucer and use the end of the sponge paint roller to apply the paint to the star shape. Don't apply too much paint to the potato, as this will make the design bleed. If you have applied too much paint, gently blot the potato on paper towels to remove the excess.

4 Begin printing onto the white paper. To ensure the design prints clearly, use a gentle rocking motion, moving the potato from side to side without lifting it from the paper. This will apply the paint evenly, even if the cut surface of the potato is not flat. Continue to print the stars at evenly spaced intervals. Allow the paint to dry completely.

gift boxes

The shape of these little gift boxes is reminiscent of the domes and finials often seen in Eastern European architecture, and the scraps of wallpaper covering them emphasize their rather exotic look. Tied with a pretty ribbon and filled with homemade candy, they would make a lovely Christmas gift.

Materials

Piece of wallpaper or sheet of
  giftwrap paper

16 x 14 in. (39 x 35 cm) piece of
  thin card

Glue stick

Tracing paper

Pencil

Scalpel or craft knife

Cutting board

¼ in. (6 mm) hole punch

Hammer

Length of ribbon

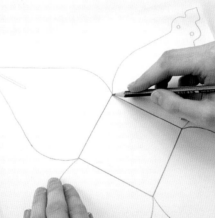

1 Stick down the piece of wallpaper or giftwrap paper onto the piece of thin card with a glue stick.

2 Copy and enlarge the box template on page 120 and transfer the outline to the card.

3 Cut out the shape carefully with the scalpel and use the hole punch and hammer to make the four holes in the tabs. Cut the slots for the tabs.

4 Score the inner lines with the scalpel where indicated to create the box shape.

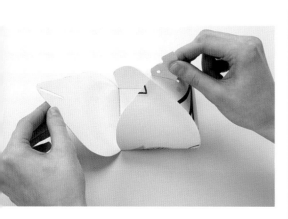

5 Place the two tabs with punched holes aligned and slot the other two sides into position.

6 Thread a ribbon through the holes and tie into a decorative bow to finish.

button & paper flowers

These little decorative flowers have a charming vintage appeal. Attach them to giftwrap or wind them around napkins and finish with a vintage lace ribbon, tied in a bow. Look out for pearl buttons in thrift shops. You could try different types of buttons; small painted glass ones would be lovely. You can find the little bells at craft suppliers.

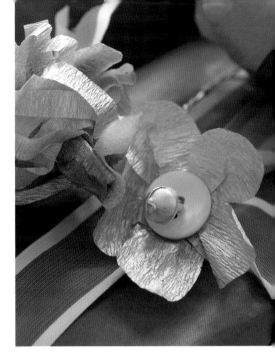

Materials

Small silver bells

Thin wire

Wire cutters

Pearl buttons

Silver crepe paper

Scissors

Glue

1 To make a button and bell flower, thread a bell onto a piece of wire approx. 8 in. (20 cm) in length. Fold the wire in half and thread a button on next, with the ends of the wire going through each of the buttonholes. Twist the wire around to secure beneath the button.

2 Cut about five small petals from the silver crepe paper and glue to the back of the button.

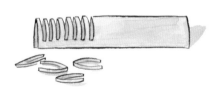

3 To make the other paper flowers, cut a length of crepe paper approx. 8¾ x 2 in. (22 x 5 cm). Fold it in half and snip along the folded edge at regular intervals to make a fringe. Make sure you do not cut down to the base of the strip.

4 Fold the strip in half and then in half again, and then roll it around a piece of wire approx. 4 in. (10 cm) in length. Secure the flowers with a small piece of wire wound around the rolled paper.

5 Cut some leaves from the silver paper and stick them to the wire stem. You could also thread on a bell or a button before winding the crepe paper around, if you like.

CHAPTER 3

gifts

lebkuchen

Lebkuchen are traditional German Christmas cookies with a good hint of ginger and spices. They can be covered with either a simple white icing or a coating of white or dark chocolate.

Ingredients

2 tablespoons clear honey

2 tablespoons molasses (black treacle)

2½ tablespoons (40 g) unsalted butter

⅓ cup (75 g) dark brown soft sugar

grated zest of ½ orange

grated zest of ½ lemon

1¾ cups (225 g) self-rising (self-raising) flour

½ teaspoon ground cinnamon

2 teaspoons ground ginger

¼ teaspoon grated nutmeg

A pinch of ground cloves

A pinch of salt

⅓ cup (50 g) ground almonds

1 egg, lightly beaten

Edible silver balls

Makes about 30

For the chocolate glaze

1 cup (175 g) dark chocolate, chopped

1 tablespoon sunflower oil

For the glacé icing

2 cups (250 g) confectioner's (icing) sugar

2–3 tablespoons water or lemon juice

Equipment

Shaped cookie cutters

2 baking sheets, lined with baking parchment

Piping bags (optional)

1 Put the honey, molasses (treacle), butter, sugar, and orange and lemon zest in a small saucepan. Set it over a low heat and stir until the butter has melted and everything is well mixed. Carefully remove from the heat and leave to cool.

2 Sift the flour, spices, and salt together into a mixing bowl, then add the ground almonds. Add the melted butter mixture and the beaten egg and mix until you get a dough.

3 To knead the dough, sprinkle a little flour on a clean work surface. Shape the dough into a ball and push on it and press it onto the work surface, turning it round often. Do this for just a minute or so until smooth, then wrap in plastic wrap (clingfilm) and chill in the fridge for at least 4 hours or overnight.

4 When you are ready to bake the Lebkuchen, preheat the oven to 350°F (180°C/Gas 4). On the floured work surface, roll the dough out to a thickness of ¼ in. (5 mm) using a rolling pin. Stamp out shapes with your cookie cutters.

5 Place the Lebkuchen on the prepared baking sheets and bake for about 15–20 minutes, or until just beginning to brown at the edges. Transfer to a wire rack to cool.

Tip

To make a quick piping bag, fill a freezer bag and snip off a corner. Fill with glaze or icing. Snip off a corner and use to pipe lines onto the Lebkuchen.

6 When the Lebkuchen are cold, make up the chocolate glaze. Put the chocolate and oil in a heatproof bowl over a pan of barely simmering water or in the microwave on a low setting. Stir very carefully until the chocolate has melted, then leave to cool for about 10 minutes before using.

7 For the glacé icing, sift the sugar into a bowl and, using a balloon whisk, gradually stir in enough water or lemon juice to make a smooth icing that will coat the back of a spoon. Add more water or juice for a runnier icing.

8 Spread chocolate glaze or glacé icing over the cookies with a palette knife or back of a spoon. Decorate with silver balls or pipe more glaze or icing over the Lebkuchen with a piping bag.

for kids: *snow globes*

Festive snow globes make great gifts for friends and family, and children really enjoy making them.

Materials

Empty, clean glass jars with lids
Sandpaper (optional)
Silver paint
Paintbrush

Strong waterproof glue or
   waterproof tile adhesive
Christmas decorations to put in jar
Pitcher (jug) and spoon for pouring
Distilled water

Glycerine
Clear dishwashing liquid
Glitter
Silicon sealant (optional)

1 Paint the lid of the jar (you may wish to sand it lightly before painting) with silver paint and let it dry completely. If required, apply a second coat of paint for better coverage and again leave to dry.

2 Use strong glue to attach the decoration to the inside of the jar lid. If the decoration is on the small side, build up a small mound using waterproof tile adhesive and press the decoration firmly into this. Leave until completely dry.

3 Use a pitcher (jug) to pour the distilled water into the jam jar. Fill it almost to the brim. Stir in two teaspoons of glycerine and half a teaspoon of washing-up liquid. Add five or six spoonfuls of glitter to the water. White or silver glitter looks most similar to snow, although bright colors like red or green can look very jolly and festive.

4 Carefully place the lid on the top of the jar and screw the lid tightly in place. The jar should be watertight, but you may wish to seal it around the edges with a thin layer of silicon sealant. Turn the jar upside down, so the Christmas decoration is the right way up.

paper-cut woodland scene

This woodland scene with the cheeky fox in the foreground has a charming folk art quality and makes a beautiful handmade gift. You can make it to fit whatever size of square frame you choose.

Materials

Tracing paper

Pencil

Sheet of white letter size (A4) paper

Cutting mat

Scalpel or craft knife

Square picture frame

Small piece of drawing (cartridge) paper

Contrasting color letter size (A4) paper

Glue stick

1 Trace the template of the tree on page 122 and transfer it to a piece of white paper. Cut the paper to the size of the picture frame, centering the tree in the square.

2 Place the paper onto a cutting mat and cut out the shapes with a sharp scalpel or craft knife.

3 Trace the template of the front fox piece on page 123 and transfer it onto the drawing (cartridge) paper. Cut out the fox section. Score the flaps and bend them back.

4 Remove the glass from the frame and place the contrast color paper into the back. Place the tree cut-out in position on top and hold in place with a couple of dabs of glue.

5 Add dabs of glue to the flaps on the front fox piece and stick in position on the bottom of the frame.

meringue snowflakes

These pretty snowflakes are simply made from a basic meringue mixture, but add a festive touch with a sprinkling of edible silver glitter or silver balls.

Ingredients

¾ cup (150 g) superfine (caster) sugar

2½ oz. (75 g) egg whites
(about 2 medium egg whites)

Edible silver glitter

Edible silver balls

Makes about 12

Equipment

Piping bag, fitted with a star-shaped tip
(nozzle)

2 solid baking sheets, lined with baking
parchment

1 Preheat the oven to 400°F (200°C/Gas 6). Tip the sugar into a small roasting pan and put it in the preheated oven for about 5 minutes until hot to the touch—be careful not to burn your fingers!

2 Turn the oven down to 225°F (110°C/Gas ¼). Place the egg whites in a large, clean mixing bowl or in the bowl of an electric mixer and beat until they are frothy.

3 Tip the hot sugar onto the egg whites in one go and continue to whisk on high speed for about 5 minutes until the meringue mixture is very stiff, white, and cold.

4 Spoon the meringue mixture into the prepared piping bag. Pipe little blobs of meringue onto the prepared baking sheets in the shape of snowflakes. Scatter silver glitter or silver balls over the top.

5 Bake in the preheated oven for about 45 minutes or until crisp and dry. Turn off the oven, leave the door closed, and let the snowflakes cool down completely inside the oven.

button bites

These tiny cookies make great stocking fillers. They are simple to make and fun to package: try sewing them onto a vintage-style button card or pop into little bags for the perfectly tailored gift.

Ingredients

½ quantity Vanilla Cookie dough (page 46)

For the ginger snap dough

1½ cups (190 g) all-purpose (plain) flour, plus extra for dusting

1 teaspoon ground ginger

½ teaspoon salt

1 teaspoon baking powder

¼ cup (60 g) unsalted butter

¼ cup (55 g) light brown sugar

1 tablespoon (20 g) molasses

1 tablespoon (20 g) light corn (golden) syrup

Makes about 35 cookies

Equipment

Round cookie cutters in assorted sizes

¼ in. (5 mm) icing tip (nozzle)

Palette knife

Baking sheet, lined with baking parchment

1 Preheat the oven to 325°F (160°C/Gas 3). To make the Ginger Snap Cookies, sift the flour, ginger, salt, and baking powder into a bowl.

2 Melt the butter, sugar, molasses, and syrup in a saucepan over a low heat until combined, then pour over the flour. Mix the butter mixture and flour together until it forms a stiff dough. Add a little more flour if the dough seems sticky. Let cool, wrap in plastic wrap (clingfilm), and refrigerate for 5 minutes.

3 Roll out the Ginger Snap dough on a surface lightly dusted with flour until about ¼ in. (5 mm) thick.

4 Use round cutters to cut out different-sized buttons. Make them quite small—between 2–3½ in. (5–8 cm) in diameter—so that they remain cute and easy to package. For each button, use the rounded end of a smaller cutter to make a neat ridge.

5 Once chilled, repeat steps 3 and 4 to roll and stamp out buttons from the Vanilla Cookie Dough.

6 Use an icing tip (nozzle) to cut two or four neat holes in each button. Push into the dough and twist slightly. Using a palette knife, lift each of the cookies onto the greased baking sheet and cool in the fridge for 5 minutes. Bake in the preheated oven for 12–15 minutes or until just golden in color.

BUTTON BITES

floral booties

These little shoes are made from linen and lined with pretty fabric, with simple embroidered bullion knots to form the charming, raised flower design. They make the perfect Christmas gift for little ones—or moms-to-be.

Materials

Scissors

Approx. 12 × 12 in. (30 × 30 cm) outer fabric, such as linen

Approx. 12 × 12 in. (30 × 30 cm) lining fabric, such as printed cotton

Embroidery needle

Blue and red embroidery floss (thread)

Pins

Sewing machine and matching thread

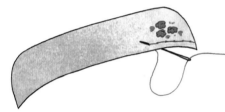

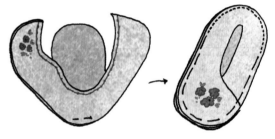

1 Copy the templates and motifs on page 123 and cut out the shapes for the upper and sole from the outer and lining fabrics. Follow the stitch guide on the template to embroider the flowers onto the outer section of the shoe (see pages 107–109 for stitch instructions). Sew the line of stitching around the top edge of the shoe, ⅝ in. (1.5 cm) down from the top. If you lay your pieces with the top edge facing you, position the flowers on the right side for the right shoe and on the opposite side for the left shoe.

2 For the right shoe, take the outer piece and lining and place them right sides together. Pin and machine stitch along the top edge, taking a ½-in. (1-cm) seam. Trim the seam allowance, turn right side out, and press.

3 Mark the center point along the bottom edge of the upper piece and the center point of the sole lining. Lay the sole lining, right side facing up, on a flat surface. Pin the upper and sole together, aligning the center points. Continue to pin the rest of the upper to the sole lining, easing the fabric around the curve and making sure that the side with the embroidery overlaps the plain side. Machine stitch around the heel section and baste (tack) the rest of the upper around the edge.

4 Position the outer sole piece over the top of the upper section. Pin and baste (tack) in place to just beyond the machine-stitched section at the heel. Machine stitch this section. Remove the basting stitches and trim the seam allowance.

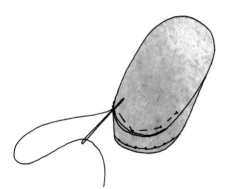

5 Turn the shoe right side out. Fold over the unstitched raw edge of the sole, to match the seam already sewn. Tuck in the raw edges of the top section and slipstitch all around the back of the heel to close the gap.

6 Repeat to make the left shoe, remembering to overlap the opposite way so that the embroidery is on the top.

bauble cookies

Festive ornament cutters are often sold in packs of 4–5 assorted shapes, ranging from the very simple to the more ornate. If you want to hang them from the Christmas tree, make a hole in the top before baking.

Ingredients

2 tablespoons light corn (golden) syrup

1 large egg yolk

1⅔ cups (200 g) all-purpose (plain) flour, plus extra for dusting

½ teaspoon baking powder

1½ teaspoons ground ginger

1 teaspoon ground cinnamon

¼ teaspoon freshly grated nutmeg

A pinch of salt

7 tablespoons (100 g) unsalted butter, chilled and diced

⅓ cup (75 g) light muscovado or light brown (soft) sugar

2–3 cups (350–500 g) royal icing sugar

Pink and violet food coloring pastes

Edible metallic balls

Assorted edible glitter

Makes 12–16

Equipment

Christmas ornament cutters

Wooden skewer or toothpick (optional)

2 solid baking sheets, lined with baking parchment

Disposable piping bags

Fine ribbon (optional)

1 Beat together the corn syrup (golden syrup) and egg yolk in a small bowl.

2 Sift the flour, baking powder, spices, and salt into a food processor (or into a mixing bowl) and add the butter. Use the pulse button to process the mixture (or rub the butter into the flour mixture with your fingertips). When the mixture starts to look like sand and there are no lumps of butter, add the sugar and pulse (or mix with your fingers) again for 30 seconds to incorporate. With the motor running, add the egg-yolk mixture and pulse (or mix with a wooden spoon) until starting to clump together.

3 Tip the mixture out onto a very lightly floured surface and knead gently to bring together into a smooth ball. Flatten the dough into a disc, wrap in plastic wrap (clingfilm), and refrigerate for 1–2 hours. Preheat the oven to 325°F (170°C/Gas 3).

4 Lightly dust a clean, dry surface with flour and roll the dough evenly to a thickness of ⅛ in. (2–3 mm). Use the cutters to stamp out as many cookies as possible from the dough, cutting each one as close as possible to the next one.

5 Arrange the cookies on the prepared baking sheets. Gather the dough scraps together, knead lightly, re-roll, and stamp out more cookies until all the dough has been used up. If you want to hang the ornaments on the Christmas tree later, use a wooden skewer or toothpick to make a hole in the top of each cookie.

6 Bake the cookies in batches on the middle shelf of the preheated oven for 10–12 minutes or until firm and lightly browned at the edges. You may need to reshape the hole for the ribbon using the skewer again. Allow the cookies to cool completely on the baking sheets before icing.

7 Use the royal icing sugar to make icing according to the packet instructions. It will need to be thick enough to hold its shape when piped, so add the water gradually until you have the correct consistency. Transfer half the icing to another bowl and tint using the pink food coloring paste. Tint the other half violet. Fill a disposable piping bag with 3 tablespoons of the pink icing. Take some of the cookies and pipe outlines around each one. Add more pink coloring paste to the remaining pink icing to make a deeper shade, if you like, and pipe outlines around more cookies.

8 Take another piping bag and spoon 3 tablespoons of the violet icing into it. Pipe an outline around the remaining cookies with the violet icing. Allow the icing to set for 10 minutes.

9 Flood the insides of the outlines with a corresponding or contrasting color. Allow to dry for 20 minutes. Pipe decorative patterns in contrasting colors on each ornament and decorate with edible silver balls and edible glitter. Allow the icing to set completely before threading with fine ribbon, if using.

polar bear hot water bottle

A cozy, covered hot water bottle makes a lovely Christmas gift, ideal for snuggling up with on the sofa and watching all those old films shown over the holidays. If your hot water bottle is a different size, make up a new template by drawing around the bottle, adding a 1-in. (2.5-cm) seam allowance to the sides and base and an extra 1½ in. (4 cm) at the top to turn down.

You will need

Hot water bottle
Tracing paper
Pencil
An old woolen sweater

Scissors
Air-erasable pen
Knitting yarn in cream or white
Embroidery needle

Black embroidery floss (thread)
Sewing machine and matching thread

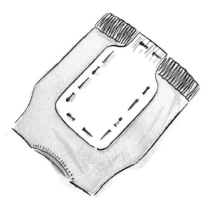

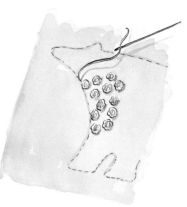

1 Place the hot water bottle on some tracing paper. Draw around it and cut out, to make a template. Pin the template to the sweater, positioning the top part of the template over the ribbed lower edge of the sweater. Cut out the back and front pieces.

2 Transfer the polar bear template on page 121 onto tracing paper. Cut it out and pin it to the front piece of the cover, positioning it approx. 6 in. (15 cm) down from the top edge and centered on the width. Draw around the shape with an air-erasable pen.

3 Fill the polar bear with bullion knots in cream yarn (see page 109). Take the yarn four times around the needle, which will make a nice rounded knot and a lovely textured surface for your polar bear.

4 Use black embroidery floss (thread) to make a bullion knot for the eye and add a few satin stitches for the nose (see page 108).

5 Pin the back and front pieces together with wrong sides facing, just at the top ribbed section. Machine sew a zig zag stitch 1½ in. (4 cm) down each seam.

Felting

Felting Before cutting out, you could felt the sweater by placing it in a very hot cycle in the washing machine but remember that the jumper will shrink, so make sure it will provide enough fabric for the front and back.

6 Turn the front and back inside out so that the right sides are together. Using zig zag stitch, sew down the sides and along the bottom edge, taking a ⅜-in. (1-cm) seam allowance. Trim any seam allowance, clip the curves, and turn right sides out.

7 Make a couple of pompoms using the cream yarn (see page 34), approx. 1¾ in. (4.5 cm) in diameter. Leave 5 in. (12 cm) of yarn attached to sew to the cover. Attach them to the side seam 1½ in. (4 cm) down at the base of the first section of zig zag. Fold the hot water bottle in half to insert it into the cover and fold over the cuff by 1½ in. (4 cm) to finish.

reindeer pillow

This pillow is embroidered with one of Santa's reindeers, but it would make a stylish addition to the living room at any time of the year. The white stitching on the soft-gray felted wool creates a particularly striking effect.

Materials

Dressmaker's carbon paper

18½ x 12¼ in. (46 x 32 cm) gray felted wool

Embroidery needle

White embroidery floss (thread) or knitting yarn

4¾ x 2 in. (12 x 5 cm) yellow felt for label

Sewing machine and matching thread

26½ x 23¼ in. (66 x 58 cm) white woolen fabric

Scissors

Pins

Pillow form (cushion pad), 12 x 20 in. (30 x 50 cm)

1 Copy the template on page 124 and, using dressmaker's carbon paper, transfer it onto the gray front piece. Center the design between the two long edges and 2¾ in. (7 cm) in from the shorter left-hand edge. Follow the stitch guide on the template and embroider the design onto the fabric (see pages 107–109 for stitch instructions).

2 To make the label, transfer the template design onto one end of the yellow felt using dressmaker's carbon paper. Follow the stitch guide to embroider the pattern. Fold the rectangle in half and machine stitch along the two side edges and outer edge of the label, keeping the stitching close to the edge.

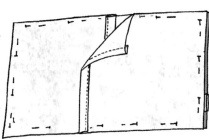
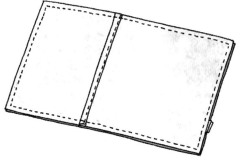

3 From the white fabric, cut one rectangle measuring 13½ x 12¼ in. (34 x 32 cm) and one measuring 12¼ x 10½ in. (32 x 26 cm). Take one piece and fold in a ½-in. (1-cm) double hem along one 12¼-in. (32-cm) edge. Pin and machine stitch the hem. Press and repeat with the other piece.

4 Place the front section with the right side facing up on your work surface. Position the two back pieces right side down, so that the hemmed edges face the center, with the larger piece overlapping. Sandwich the label with the design facing down, in between the front and back section on the side edge. Pin in position so that the label edge aligns with the raw edges of the pillow.

5 Machine stitch all around the edge of the pillow, taking a ½-in. (1-cm) seam. Trim the seam allowance and snip across each corner. Turn right side out through the envelope back and press. Insert the pillow form (cushion pad).

chocolate money

Here is a great way to make money… well, the edible kind!
Milk and dark chocolate money gilded with an edible golden
luster makes a great festive gift for the guys.

Ingredients

3½ oz. (100 g) white chocolate

8 oz. (225 g) milk or dark chocolate

Edible glue

Edible gold luster

Equipment

Paintbrushes

Plastic nozzle bottle

Chocolate coin mold

Waxed (greaseproof) paper

Makes about 20 chocolates

1 Melt the white chocolate in a bowl set over a pan of hot water, making sure the bottom of the bowl does not come into contact with the water, then let cool slightly. Use a nozzle bottle to fill the face on the coin with the melted white chocolate. Tap the mold gently and refrigerate for 15 minutes. Meanwhile, melt the dark or milk chocolate in a bowl and, once the white chocolate has cooled, fill the remainder of the coin mold using either a nozzle bottle or a small pitcher (jug). Gently tap the mold and refrigerate for at least 30 minutes.

2 If you would prefer, you could use only one type of chocolate to fill the mold. In this case, only melt your preferred chocolate (dark, milk, or white) and fill the coin mold using either a nozzle bottle or a small pitcher (jug). You will not need to refrigerate the chocolate after filling in the face. Once the mold has been filled, as before, gently tap the mold to release any air and refrigerate for at least 40 minutes.

3 When the chocolate has cooled and solidified, gently push out the chocolate coins onto a sheet of waxed (greaseproof) paper. Use a paintbrush to paint a small amount of edible glue onto the coin. With a clean dry brush, gently tap on the edible gold luster. Leave to set.

gingerbread doorstop

There are many doorstops in the shape of houses available to buy, but this gingerbread house is much more unusual. Use brown polka-dot fabric for the gingerbread, with rickrack braid for the frosting (icing). Pretty buttons in candy colors on the roof add a suitably sweet finishing touch. A practical version of the edible house on page 14!

Materials

29½ x 16 in. (75 x 40 cm) medium-weight iron-on interfacing

Scissors

29½ x 16 in. (75 x 40 cm) fabric

Pins

Sewing needle and matching thread

Sewing machine

27½ in. (70 cm) white jumbo rikrak

28½ in. (70 cm) velvet ribbon, ¼ in. (5 mm) wide

4-in. (10-cm) square of brown felt

3⅝ x 1⅝ in. (9 x 4 cm) pink felt

16 in. (40 cm) white medium rikrak

Polyester toy filling or kapok

Dried peas or similar

8 x 7⅝ in. (20 x 19 cm) white felt

15 in. (38 cm) pink and green medium rikrak

12 buttons, approx. ⅝ in. (1.5 cm) in diameter

Fast-drying high-tack fabric glue

1 Following the manufacturer's instructions, apply interfacing to the wrong side of the fabric. Enlarge the templates on page 125 by 200 percent and cut out. Cut two side pieces, one front, one back, two roof pieces, and one base.

2 To make a tab for the chimney, cut a strip of fabric measuring 3⅝ x 2¾ in. (9 x 7 cm). Fold it in half lengthwise, right sides together, and machine stitch along the long raw edge. Press the seam open. Turn the strip right side out and press, with the seam running down the center of one side. Fold the tab in half widthwise, with the seam on the inside. Aligning the raw edges, pin, and baste (tack) it onto one long edge of one roof piece. Pin and machine stitch the second roof piece to the first, along the edge with the tab. Press the seam open.

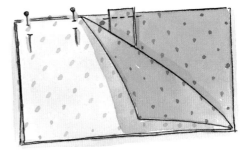

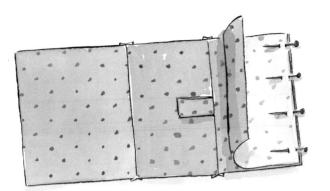

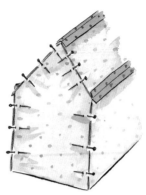

3 With right sides together, pin and machine stitch the front to one long raw edge of the roof. Press the seam open. Stitch the back to the other long raw edge of the roof and press the seam open.

4 With right sides together, pin and machine stitch the side panels to the front/roof/back section, matching the corners of the base with the seams of the house. Machine stitch in place, starting and finishing ⅜ in. (1 cm) from the edges and making a snip at each corner as you go. Turn right side out and press.

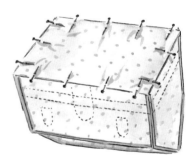

5 Pin and machine stitch the length of jumbo rikrak braid all around the right side of the house, ¾ in. (2 cm) from the bottom edge, overlapping the ends slightly and folding the top layer under at the back of the house. Pin and machine stitch the velvet ribbon just above the rikrak, again overlapping the ends and folding the top layer under.

6 Using the patterns on page 125, cut out paper patterns for the door, heart, and windows. Cut one door and two large windows from brown felt and two small windows and a heart from pink felt. Using small straight stitches, hand stitch the pink windows onto the brown windows and the heart to the door. Using running stitch, hand stitch the white medium rikrak braid around the arch of the windows and the door, then stitch the windows and door onto the front of the house.

7 Turn the house wrong side out. With right sides together, aligning the corners of the base with the seams of the house, pin the base in place. Machine stitch, starting and finishing ⅜ in. (1 cm) from the edges, making a snip at each corner as you sew and leaving a 3-in. (7-cm) gap along the back edge. Turn the house right side out and press.

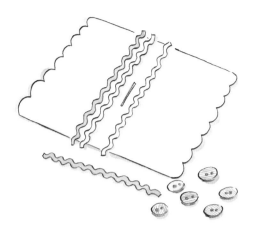

8 Fill the house about three-quarters full with polyester toy filling or kapok, then fill the remaining space with dried peas or similar. Handstitch the gap in the base closed.

9 Using the pattern on page 125, cut a frosting (icing) roof from white felt. Cut a slit for the tab chimney where indicated. Cut the pink and green rikrak in half. Pin and machine stitch one strip of each color to the felt roof on either side of the slit, folding the ends neatly to the wrong side. Sew six buttons to each side of the felt roof. Apply glue to the roof of the house and slip the felt roof over the chimney. Hold in place until the glue is dry.

Techniques

Transferring Patterns and Motifs

All templates on pages 110–123 are reproduced at 100 percent, unless otherwise stated. To transfer the templates, draw around them onto tracing paper using a soft pencil, including any fold lines or stitch patterns. Place the trace over a sheet of paper or card, pencil side down. Draw over the outline with a hard pencil, pressing hard to transfer the mark. Redraw the transferred line, if necessary, then cut out your paper or card template and use as directed. You can either trace directly from the book, or photocopy the page first. If necessary enlarge any templates on a photocopier before tracing.

If you are using your template to cut fabric or transfer an embroidery pattern or motif onto fabric, you can use an air-erasable pen or a dressmaker's fade-away marker pen.

If you are transferring the template or pattern to a thick or dark fabric, lay dressmaker's carbon paper on the fabric, carbon side down. Lay the embroidery pattern on top and trace over the motif with a ballpoint pen. You can buy carbon paper in different colors suitable for different fabrics.

Basting (tacking)

This is a temporary way of holding two or more pieces of fabric together before stitching, if pins would get in the way. It's useful when making seams in awkward corners, or when sewing curved edges together, or when another layer will be added on top and you wouldn't be able to get to the pins.

To baste (tack) by hand, sew long running stitches and don't secure the thread at the end; when you want to remove the basting (tacking), just snip off the knot at the start of the thread, and pull the other end.

Machine Stitching

The key to successful machine stitching is to stitch slowly and in a straight line. Learn to control the speed so that the machine doesn't run away with you!

Straight machine stitch is used for seams; set a stitch length of 10–12 on a scale of 1–20, and a stitch width of 0.

Zig zag stitching is used for finishing seam allowances to stop them from fraying and to create a satin-stitch effect in machine embroidery. The stitch width varies depending on the fabric and the desired effect.

Hand Stitches

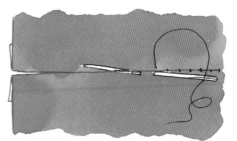

Slip Stitch

Slip stitch is used to close openings—for example, when you've left a gap in a seam in order to turn a piece right side out—and to appliqué one piece of fabric to another. Work from right to left. Slide the needle between the two pieces of fabric, bringing it out on the edge of the top fabric so that the knot in the thread is hidden between the two layers. Pick up one or two threads from the base fabric, then bring the needle up a short distance along, on the edge of the top fabric, and pull through. Repeat to the end.

Straight Stitch

Straight stitches can be arranged to form other embroidery stitches, such as seed stitch and star stitch (see right).

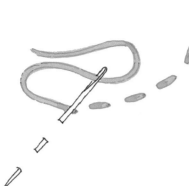

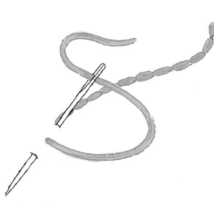

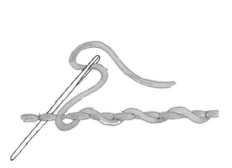

Running Stitch

Work from right to left. Secure the thread with a couple of small stitches, and then make several small stitches by bringing the needle up and back down through the fabric several times along the stitching line. Pull the needle through and repeat. Try to keep the stitches and the spaces between them the same size.

Backstitch

Work from right to left. Bring the needle up from the back of the fabric, one stitch length to the left of the end of the stitching line. Insert it one stitch length to the right, at the very end of the stitching line, and bring it up again one stitch length in front of the point from which it first emerged. Pull the thread through. To begin the next stitch, insert the needle at the left-hand end of the previous stitch. Continue to the end.

Whipped Backstitch

Work a line of backstitches (see left). Using a blunt needle, slide the needle under the thread of the first backstitch from top to bottom and pull the thread through. Repeat the process in each stitch in the row.

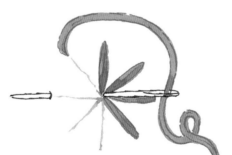

French Knot

Bring the needle up from the back of the fabric to the front. Wrap the thread two or three times around the tip of the needle, then reinsert the needle at the point where it first emerged, holding the wrapped threads with the thumbnail of your non-stitching hand, and pull the needle all the way through. The wraps will form a small knot on the surface of the fabric.

Star Stitch

Work a series of straight stitches from the outside of a circle to the center point to create a star shape. If you wish, you can further embellish this stitch by working a French knot (see right) at each point of the "star."

Seed Stitch

Work pairs of very short straight stitches, positioning them randomly to fill an area.

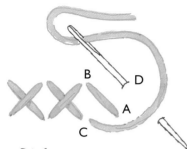

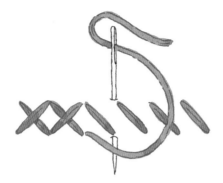

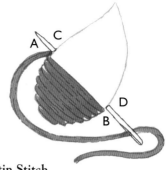

Cross Stitch

To work a single cross stitch, bring the needle up at A and down at B, then up at C and down at D.

To work a row of cross stitches, work the diagonal stitches in one direction only, from right to left, then reverse the direction and work the second half of the stitch across each stitch made on the first journey.

Satin Stitch

This is a "filling" stitch that is useful for motifs such as flower petals and leaves. Work from left to right. Draw the shape on the fabric, then work straight stitches across it, coming up at A and down at B, then up at C and down at D, and so on. Place the stitches next to each other, so that no fabric can be seen between them. You can also work a row of backstitch around the edge to define the outline more clearly.

Chain stitch

Bring the needle out at the end of the stitching line. Re-insert it at the same point and bring it out a short distance away, looping the thread around the needle tip. Pull the thread through. To begin the next stitch, insert the needle at the point at which it last emerged, just inside the loop of the previous chain, and bring it out a short distance away, again looping the thread around the needle tip. Repeat to continue.

Detached Chain Stitch

Work a single chain, as left, but fasten it by taking a small vertical stitch across the bottom of the loop.

Daisy Stitch

Work a group of six to eight detached chain stitches in a circle to form a flower shape.

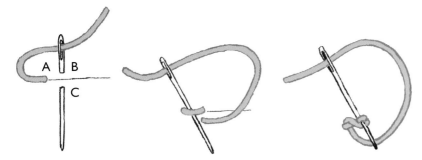
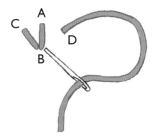

Palestrina Stitch

Bring the needle to the front of the fabric at A. Put the needle in above the line at B and bring it out below the line at C. Take the needle under the stitch from the top to the bottom without catching the fabric. Pull through gently.

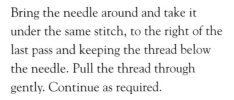

Bring the needle around and take it under the same stitch, to the right of the last pass and keeping the thread below the needle. Pull the thread through gently. Continue as required.

Fern Stitch

Bring the needle to the front of the fabric at A and put it in at B. Bring the needle out at C and put it in at B. Then bring it out again at D and again put it in at B to complete the stitch. Bring the needle out just below B to continue.

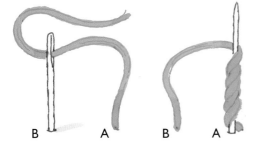
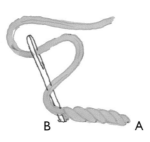

Bullion Knot

This is similar to a French knot (see page 107), but creates a longer coil of thread rather than a single knot. Bring the needle up at A and take it down at B, leaving a loose loop of thread—the distance from A to B being the length of knot that you require. Bring the needle back up at A and wrap the thread

around the needle five to eight times, depending on how long you want the knot to be. Hold the wrapped thread in place with your left hand and pull the needle all the way through. Insert the needle at B and pull through, easing the coiled stitches neatly into position.

Templates

Some of the templates will need to be enlarged and the easiest way is on a photocopier—the percentage enlargement you will need is given. See page 106 for copying instructions.

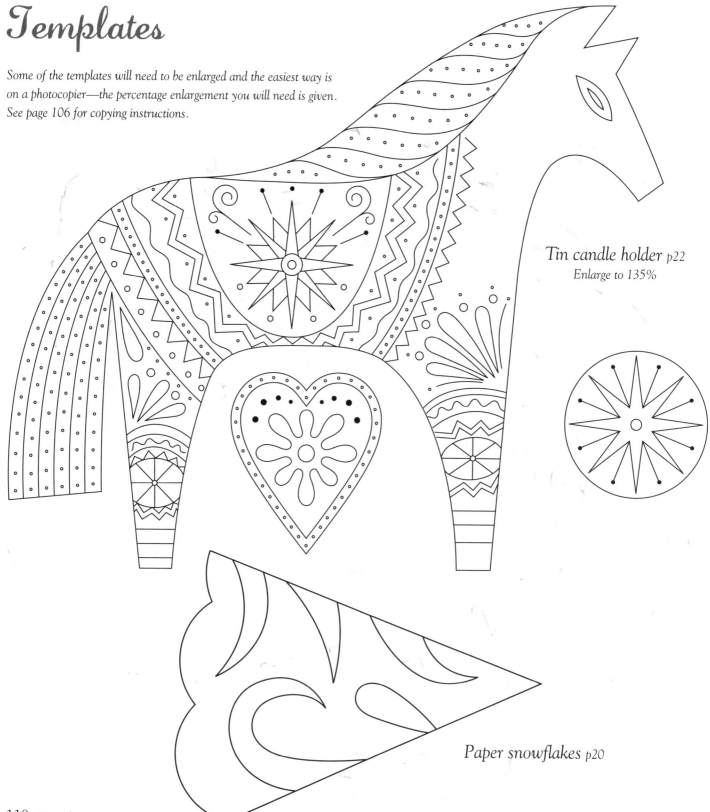

Tin candle holder p22
Enlarge to 135%

Paper snowflakes p20

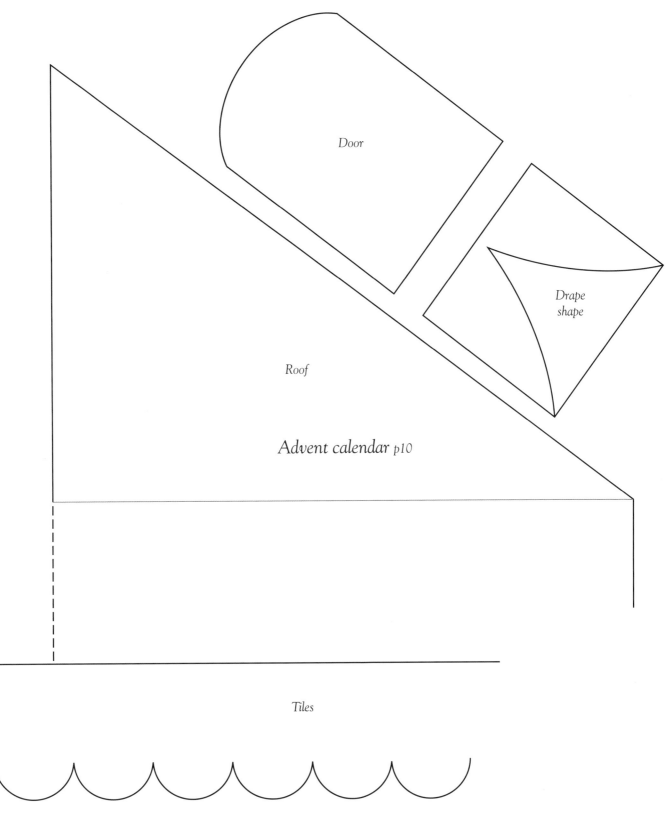

Door

Drape
shape

Roof

Advent calendar *p10*

Tiles

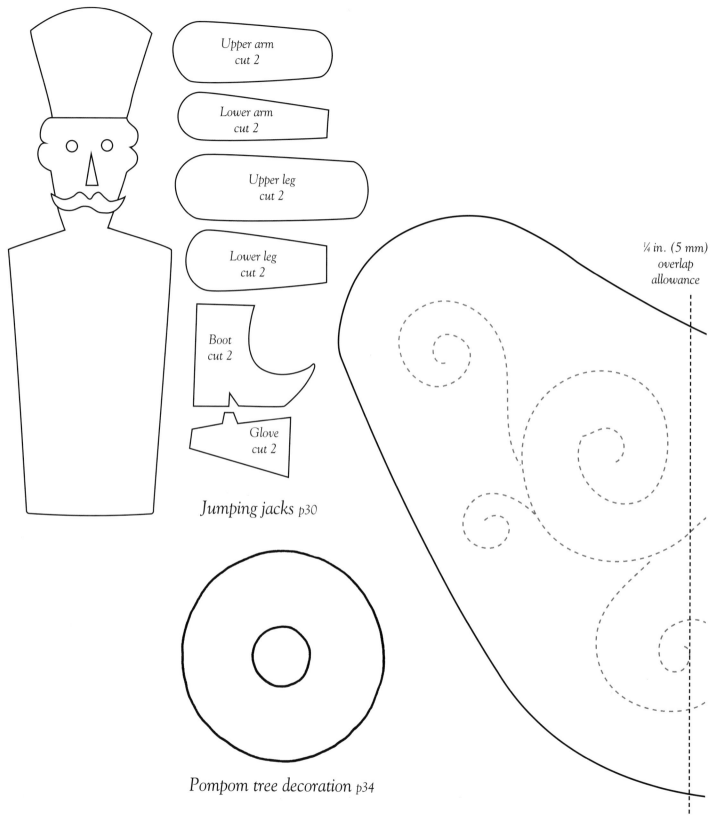

Upper arm
cut 2

Lower arm
cut 2

Upper leg
cut 2

Lower leg
cut 2

Boot
cut 2

Glove
cut 2

Jumping jacks p30

¼ in. (5 mm)
overlap
allowance

Pompom tree decoration p34

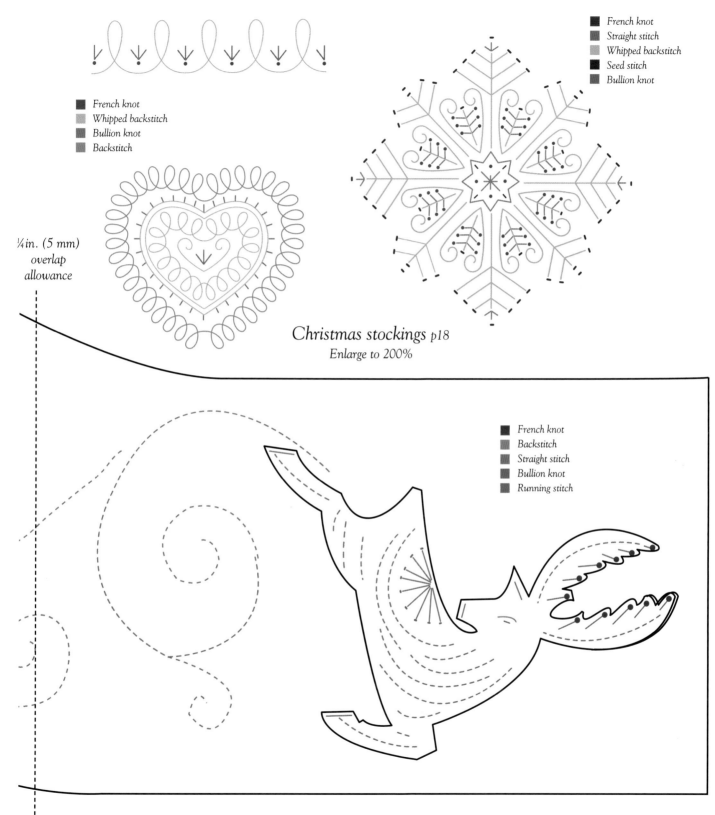

French knot
Whipped backstitch
Bullion knot
Backstitch

French knot
Straight stitch
Whipped backstitch
Seed stitch
Bullion knot

¼ in. (5 mm)
overlap
allowance

Christmas stockings *p18*
Enlarge to 200%

French knot
Backstitch
Straight stitch
Bullion knot
Running stitch

¼ in. (5 mm) overlap
allowance

Tin bird clips p38

Snowflake garland p40

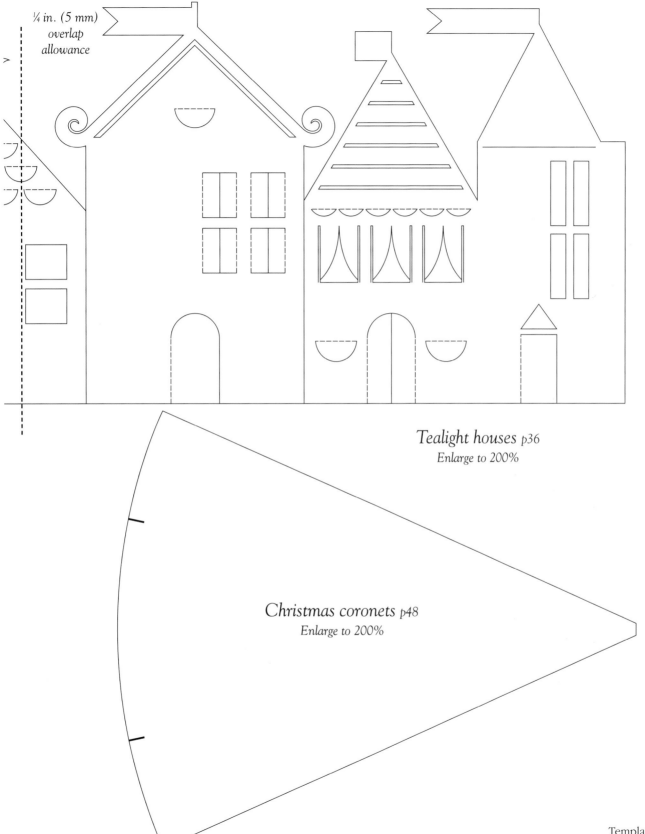

¼ in. (5 mm)
overlap
allowance

Tealight houses p36
Enlarge to 200%

Christmas coronets p48
Enlarge to 200%

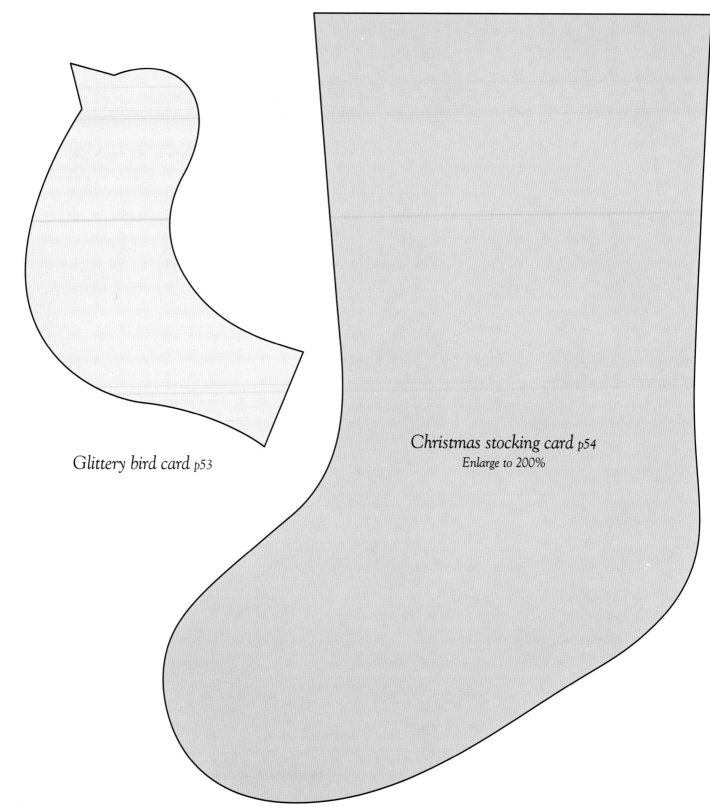

Glittery bird card *p53*

Christmas stocking card *p54*
Enlarge to 200%

Rubber-stamped cards p60

Robin's nest card p57

Patchwork wrap and card p69

Embroidery gift tags p64

■ French knot
■ Backstitch
■ Straight stitch
∥ Star stitch
■ Seed stitch
■ Cross stitch

Goody bags and labels p66

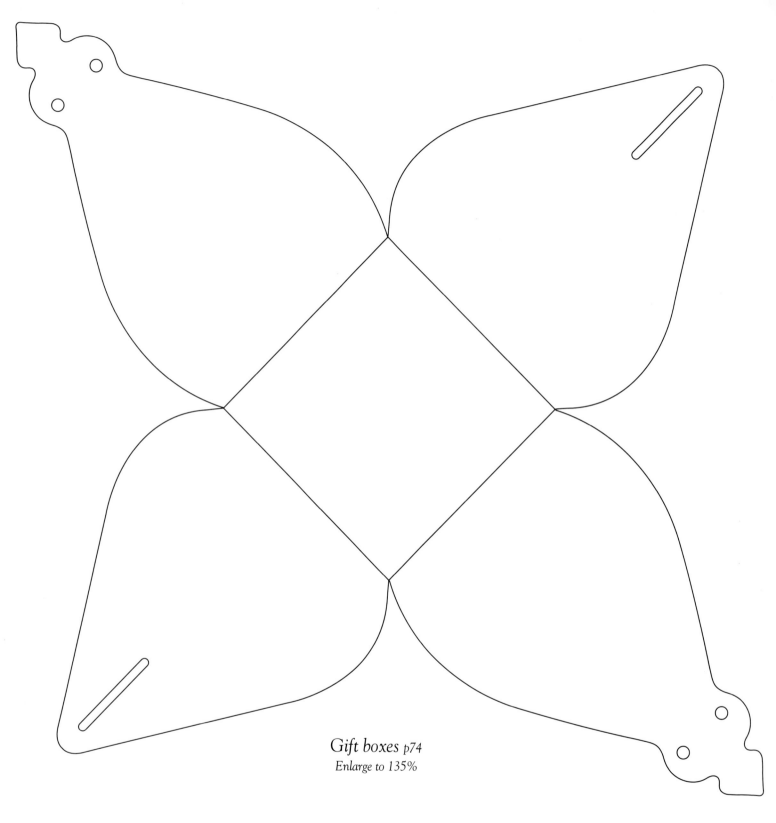

Gift boxes p74
Enlarge to 135%

Polar bear hot water bottle p94

Paper cut woodland scene p84

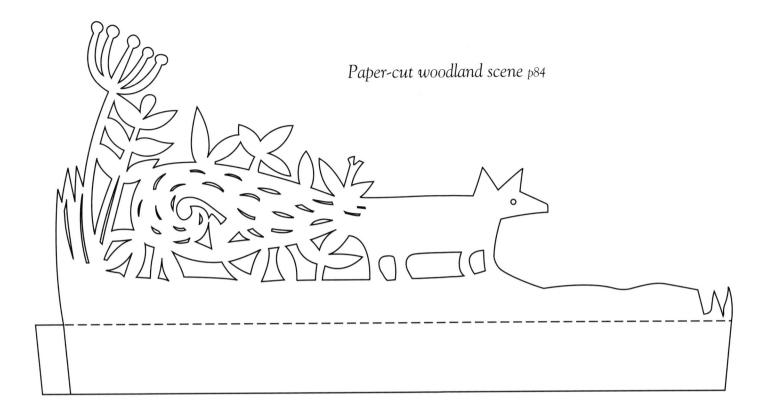

Paper-cut woodland scene p84

Floral booties p90

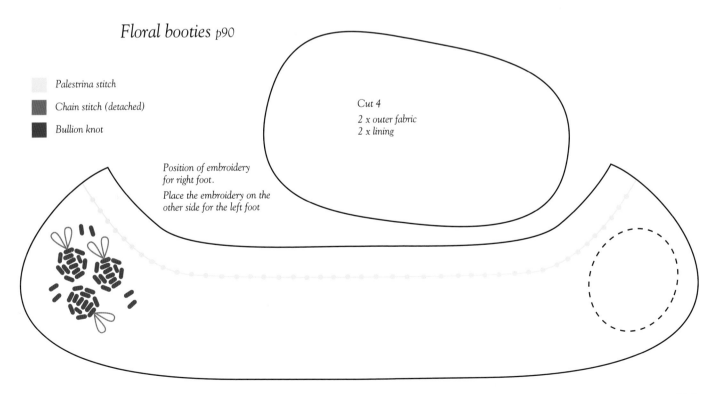

Palestrina stitch

Chain stitch (detached)

Bullion knot

Cut 4
2 x outer fabric
2 x lining

*Position of embroidery
for right foot.*

*Place the embroidery on the
other side for the left foot*

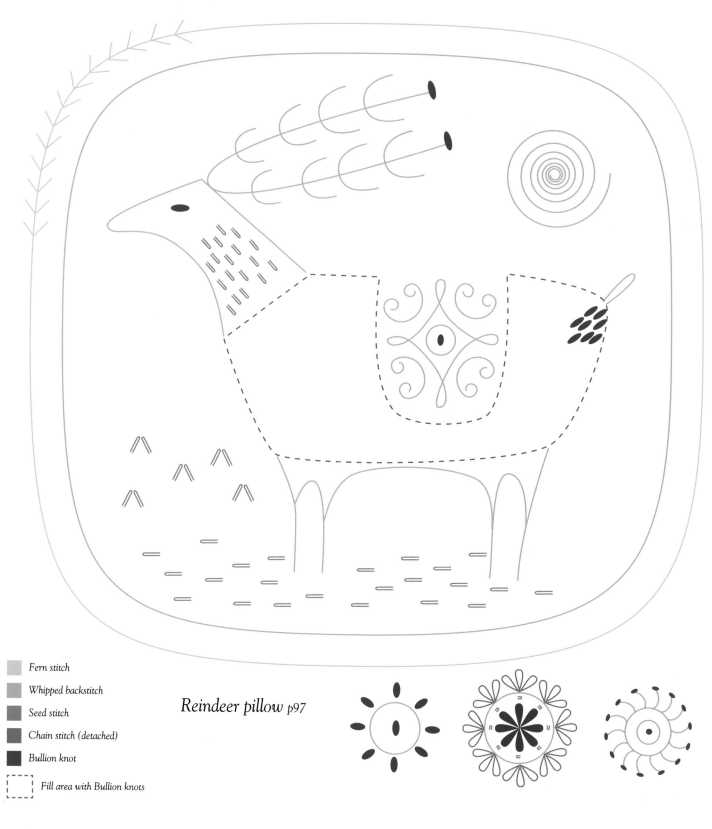

Fern stitch

Whipped backstitch

Seed stitch

Chain stitch (detached)

Bullion knot

Fill area with Bullion knots

Reindeer pillow p97

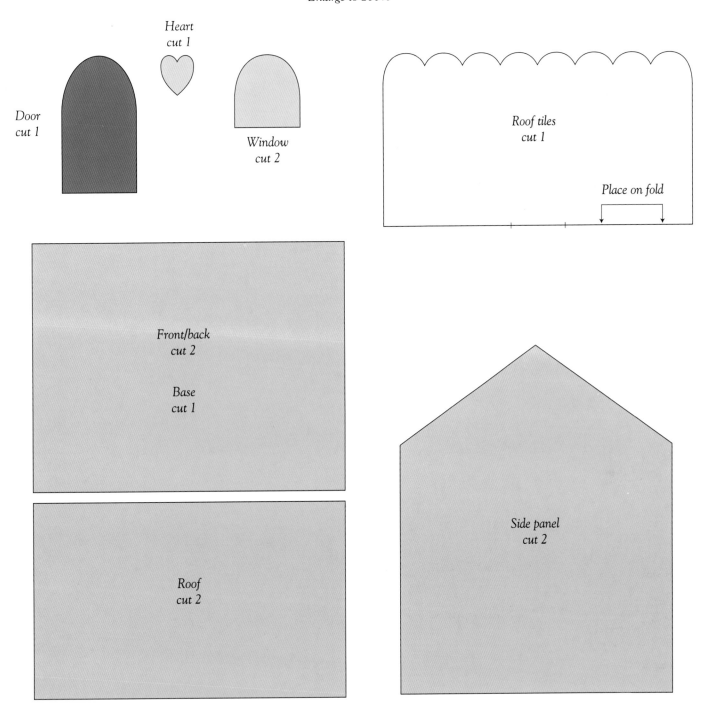

Gingerbread doorstop *p102*

Enlarge to 200%

Heart
cut 1

Door
cut 1

Window
cut 2

Roof tiles
cut 1

Place on fold

Front/back
cut 2

Base
cut 1

Side panel
cut 2

Roof
cut 2

Resources

US SUPPLIERS

A.C. Moore
Stores nationwide
1-888-226-6673
www.acmoore.com

Art Supplies Online
Online store
1-800-967-7367
www.artsuppliesonline.com

Britex Fabrics
146 Geary Street
San Francisco, CA 94108
415-392-2910
www.britexfabrics.com

Buy Fabrics
8967 Rand Avenue
Daphne, Al 36526
877-625-2889
www.buyfabrics.com

Cia's Palette
4155 Grand Avenue S
Minneapolis, MN 55409
612-229-5227
www.ciaspalette.com

Crafts, etc.
Online store
1-800-888-0321
www.craftsetc.com

Craft Site Directory
Useful online resource
www.craftsitedirectory.com

Fabricland/Fabricville

Over 170 stores in Canada
www.fabricland.com
www.fabricville.com

Hobby Lobby
Stores nationwide
www.hobbylobby.com

J & O Fabrics
9401 Rt. 130
Pennsauken, NJ 08110
856-663-2121
www.jandofabrics.com

Jo-Ann Fabric and Craft Store
Stores nationwide
1-888-739-4120
www.joann.com

Kate's Paperie
Stores across New York
1-800-809-9880
www.katespaperie.com

Michaels
Stores nationwide
1-800-642-4235
www.michaels.com

Paper Source
Stores nationwide
www.paper-source.com

Tinsel Trading Company
823 Lexington Ave.
New York, NY 10065
212-730-1030
www.tinseltrading.com

UK SUPPLIERS

Blooming Felt
www.bloomingfelt.co.uk

The Cloth House
47 Berwick Street
London W1F 8SL
020 7437 5155
www.clothhouse.com

Dots n Stripes
www.dotsnstripes.co.uk

John Lewis
Stores nationwide
08456 049 049
www.johnlewis.com

MacCulloch and Wallis
25–26 Dering Street
London WIS 1AT
020 7629 0311
www.macculloch-wallis.co.uk

Paperchase
www.paperchase.co.uk
0161 839 1500
]
V V Rouleaux
102 Marylebone Lane
London W1U 2QD
020 7224 5179
www.vvrouleaux.com

Index

Credits

Project credits:

Emma Hardy Glittery bird card, Christmas stocking card, Gingerbread doorstop.

Annie Rigg Marzipan Christmas figures, Gingerbread house, Lebkuchen, Gingerbread ornaments, Meringue snowflakes.

Laura Tabor Button bites, Chocolate money, Stained glass cookies.

Mia Underwood Christmas coronets.

Catherine Woram Pompom decorations, Felt motif cards, Potato print giftwrap, Snowglobes.

Clare Youngs Advent calendar, Christmas stockings, Paper snowflakes, Tin candle holders, Tassel decorations, Jumping jacks, Tealight houses, Tin bird clip wreath, Snowflake garland, Christmas crackers, Robin's nest card, Rubber stamped cards, Embroidered gift tags, Goody bags and labels, Gift boxes, Button and paper flowers, Patchwork wrap and card, Polar bear hot water bottle cover, Paper cut woodland scene, Floral booties, Reindeer pillow.

Photography credits:

Caroline Arber pp 90–91, 97–99, 25–27, 30–33

Tara Fisher pp 92–93

Jo Henderson pp 48–49

Lisa Linder pp 28–29, 24–27, 80–81, 86–87

Martin Norris (step photography) pp 20–21, 36–37, 57–59, 74–76, 84–85

Debbie Patterson pp 102–105

Claire Richardson pp 64–65, 18–19, 20–21, 36–37,57–59, 74–76, 84–85

Claire Richardson and James Gardiner pp 10–13, 22–24, 38–39, 40–42, 43–45, 60–61, 66–68, 77–78, 69–71, 94–96

Tino Tedaldi pp 52–53, 54–56

Stuart West pp 88–89, 100–101

Polly Wreford pp 34–35, 62–63, 72–73, 82–83